Rewild or Die

Rewild or Die

*Revolution and Renaissance
at the End of Civilization*

Urban Scout

Edition 1.1 (2016)
First published 2008.

ISBN: 978-1-62106-972-0

Book design by George Steel [george.steel@gmail.com].

Cover photo *Right time, wrong place* by Kristaps Bergfelds
[https://www.flickr.com/photos/narciss/2441820204].
Dandelion motif adapted from drawing by Karl Urban
[https://openclipart.org/detail/57355/].
Figure 1 inspired by diagram in *Managing Michigan Wildlife: A
Landowner's Guide*
[http://www.dnr.state.mi.us/publications/pdfs/
huntingwildlifehabitat/Landowners_Guide/].

Acknowledgments

I would first and foremost like to acknowledge the largest influences on my thoughts and work: Daniel Quinn, Tom Brown Jr., Derrick Jensen, Martín Prechtel, Joseph Campbell, Toby Hemenway, Jean Liedloff, M. Kat Anderson, Nancy Turner, Jason Godesky, and Willem Larsen. Without their words I would not understand the workings of civilization or walk the path of rewilding. I will forever live in debt to them.

Secondly I want to thank my friends Lisa Wells, Nicholas Often, Brandon Rubesh, Jeff Packard, and Nancy and Matt Fitzgerald (may they rest in peace). Without their collective support I wouldn't have become myself and certainly wouldn't have made it through my teenage years. I will forever live in debt to them.

Thirdly I want to thank my family for supporting me and understanding me. I could not do what I do without their unconditional support and love. I will forever live in debt to them.

Fourth, I want to send my thanks to the Earth, the water, the fungi and plants, the insects and animals, the trees, the birds, the wind, the clouds, the sun, moon, and stars for talking to me even when I stopped listening. I will forever live in debt to them.

Lastly I want to thank my muse. The invisible force(s?) that makes me do what I do and whispers ideas in my ear. To the real Urban Scout, I send my biggest thanks. I will forever live in debt to you.

Special thanks to George Steel, who spent hours nagging me to put *Rewild or Die* back out into the world, and who dedicated hours of formatting to make it look more professional. Huge thanks to Mindy Fitch, who copyedited this second edition.

Foreword

Hi and welcome to the second edition of *Rewild or Die*, Urban Scout's anti-civilization manifesto!

At some point I gave up on this project and began a complete rewrite, but I'm not sure if I'll ever finish that, as I abandoned the Urban Scout project in favor of my non-profit Rewild Portland, which now consumes the majority of my time and energy. I was also a bit embarrassed about the quality of *Rewild or Die*, in that it was full of typos (granted it is also written in an experimental version of English). But still. I was nervous that my affiliation as Urban Scout (a bridge-burning asshole, critic, and blogger) would affect my ability to build relationships that would help Rewild Portland grow. I don't agree with everything Urban Scout said or did; in fact I'm not really even that into his voice anymore. BUT, two words: George Steel. My friend George Steel just wouldn't allow me to kill *Rewild or Die*. He demanded that I keep it up. I told him that if I were to put it back up, it would need to be seriously copy edited and slightly edited for content. He said he could do the typeface, but I needed an editor. I'm a broke environmental educator working three jobs and don't have the money to pay a professional copy editor. Luckily I met Mindy Fitch, a professional copy editor, and was able to convince her to edit my book. Without those two, I would have let this project continue to fade away.

It's strange reflecting back on the totality and various iterations of my Urban Scout project. It's been years since I donned a loincloth and took to the streets to light bowdrill fires, years since I wrote an angry, caffeine-enraged blog. Urban Scout is gone for now. So what happened? Where did he go? Longtime readers often ask me this question. In brief I say that Urban Scout was a moniker, a muse, and

I've moved on. But this feels unsatisfactory to me, so I'll go into more detail.

Urban Scout started out as a fictional character created by me and a friend. He was the protagonist in a short film we made during the summer of 2003. He became more of an alter ego and muse for me in late 2004 as the film wrapped up, and from there he turned into a blog and persona. My blog was originally titled *The Adventures of Urban Scout*. I wrote that Urban Scout was "part fact/part fiction, part man/part myth." I said that I tried "to use the comedic irony and novelty of our situation as a clever disguise to cloak and spread a truly sustainable worldview, for a time beyond our own." The blog and online persona were very active from about 2006 to 2009. By 2011 I wasn't writing much anymore, and my *Rewild or Die* book tour in the spring of that year was sort of a swan song for Urban Scout. From time to time I hear his voice in my head, and it feels like I have to hold him back. It's not really me, but it's something deeper that speaks through me from a far-off place. That's all I can really say about that.

Looking back now is weird. I had to get my own identity back, learn to interpret what Urban Scout says and filter it through my own head rather than just give him the reins. I'm able to take what he says and feels and translate it into something more broadly "appealing." However, that's not particularly my goal. My goal since 2000 has been to actively create a rewilding community in Portland, Oregon, through Rewild Portland. Urban Scout has helped me clarify my own purpose and understand the power of the muse. I'm too sensitive, though. Urban Scout doesn't give a darn what people think, really. But since we share the same body, or rather because I let him use my body and mind as a vehicle, I get blamed for his assholery. My heart just can't take it anymore. I'm a nice person and

I want people to like me. I had to shut him up because his spirit is one of "truth speaking," and generally people don't want to hear the truth, especially when it comes from an angry-sounding dude. Now that I don't give my muse total creative control (so to speak), I feel much happier, and I've made a lot more headway in creating the kind of life I want to live.

I look back at the Urban Scout years with fondness, but as I read these chapters I realize I'll never really be happy with *Rewild or Die*, in part because I do not feel as though I wrote it. It is Urban Scout's book. My new book on the same topic, if I manage to finish it, will be vastly different from his. I am tentatively calling it *Rewild and Live*.

Peter Michael Bauer, October 2015

A Quick Preface

I didn't write this book to change people's minds about civilization, or to stand as "the word" of rewilding, or to prove to the civilized that a horticulturalist or hunter-gatherer way of life works better for people and the planet than the devastating effects of agricultural civilization (okay, maybe a little). Many other books exist on those topics, full of wide-ranging archaeological, historical, ecological, and anthropological evidence (see my bibliography!). With this book, I intend to clarify the meaning behind this cultural renaissance we call rewilding. I do this through sharing my experiences and thoughts on rewilding in an attempt to shed light on elements of rewilding that some may not have seen.

The thoughts in this book reflect my current level of experience and collection of evidence as of 2008. My thoughts on these topics will most likely change over time with new experiences and different pieces of evidence. Honestly, I don't agree all that much with some of the things I've written here. But I feel getting the ideas into the world outweighs any hesitations for publishing this work. I could write a whole Literacy vs. Rewilding chapter about how the written word, like the verb *to be* (see "English vs. Rewilding"), plays god by not allowing things to change the way they did in oral cultures. But maybe I'll save that for another book.

Blah, blah, blah. That said, I have gleaned a lot of information and had countless experiences with rewilding in my life. Though I don't claim expertise, I will stake my claim for the experience I do have! This book works as a tally of my experiences and accumulated thoughts on rewilding. Love it or leave it.

Contents

Rewilding: An Introduction

Rewild, *verb*: to return to a more natural or wild
state; the process of undoing domestication

The first time I saw the word *rewilding*, it grabbed me
immediately. I knew that at long last I had a word to
describe what I do. For a decade I had used many words attempting to describe my lifestyle: wilderness survivalist,
primitivist, anti-civilizationist, tracker, naturalist, perma-
culturalist, environmentalist, green anarchist, anarcho-
primitivist... The list went on and on. Nothing quite fit
until I found *rewilding*.

No other word I've found encompasses the act of abandoning civilization and its roots in domestication like *rewild*.
It also struck me because, as a verb, it implies an action, a
process, rather than an end point. An obvious premise
sits in this word: giving something back its wildness.
Wildness means a lot of different things to a lot of different
people. But let's go with dictionary.com's definition:

Wild, *adjective*:

1. Living in a state of nature; not tamed or domesticated: a wild animal: *wild geese*
2. Growing or produced without cultivation or
   the care of humans, as plants, flowers, fruit, or
   honey: *wild cherries*

3. Uncultivated, uninhabited, or waste: *wild country*
4. Uncivilized or barbarous: *wild tribes*

Combine that with:

> **Re:** a prefix, occurring originally in loanwords from Latin, used with the meaning "again" or "again and again" to indicate repetition, or with the meaning "back" or "backward" to indicate withdrawal or backward motion: regenerate; refurbish; retype; retrace; revert

Considering these definitions, particularly the first entry for wild ("living in a state of nature"), it makes sense to define rewilding as a return to a more natural state.

Why do definitions matter? People must have a shared reality in order to work together in that reality. I once got into the most insane argument with a man who refused to share reality with me, claiming that "nothing is real" and "there is no such thing as facts." These arguments looked more like philosophical masturbation than practical thinking that would lead to taking actions to create a sustainable planet. While I agreed in the philosophical sense with him, it didn't help anyone to make choices about their actions, and to make those actions in the real world. While I don't believe in the concept of "facts," I do believe that we can agree on *shared observations of reality*. We can observe that agriculture destroys the soil. If we can't share that reality, we can't work together to change our subsistence strategy to one that builds soil. Similarly, if we can't share a reality of what it means to rewild, the word might as well mean nothing at all. The more clearly we define an idea, the easier time we will have using it for practical purposes.

In a sense, I will claim ownership of the term rewilding, in that my life's work centers around caretaking the idea of what it means to return to a wild, undomesticated life. That, to me, means a hunter-gatherer lifestyle *in its wholeness*. I don't think of rewilding as some new buzzword or some small scene of people or a just wildlife conservation tactic. I see it as a complex lens through which I view the world. This lens helps me to make decisions about how to live my life.

Now, some contention may lie in that I strongly advocate against running away to the wilderness (which most people assume rewilding implies). While I strongly advocate against it, I still see it as part of rewilding. Because my focus lies in fostering as much rewilding as possible, running away to the wilderness doesn't effect much change or create the hunter-gatherer lifestyle in its wholeness. It doesn't mean it doesn't have its own merit: it certainly does! I also advocate for creating "rewilding havens," land where people can work together to rewild. This differs from running away into the wilderness because people still have an interface with civilization to draw out its members, rather than shunning all of it and living as a hermit (which I believe also has its own merit).

When it comes down to it, though, I don't see one "right" way to rewild. Everyone has their own limits and passions. I will continue to do what I can to build a cultural momentum of rewilding, using the fullest extent and articulation of the practical, shared definition. This shared definition gives us a clear shared goal to work toward.

The more I talk with people and read and write about rewilding, the more I find that the above definition appears oversimplified for an average member of civilization. Most people have preconceived notions of the words *wild*, *natural*, and *domesticated* that stem from civilization's mythology, which means the definitions serve the purpose of convincing people to believe in civilization. This means that when an average person reads or hears the above definition they will not understand what rewilding actually means to someone who has redefined those concepts (outside of civilization's propaganda). Therefore, the definition can obscure more than it reveals unless we simultaneously redefine several other concepts.

Now you see why I get a headache trying to explain rewilding in a couple of paragraphs. The definition begs a more complex analysis. For example, what does a wild state actually look like (compared to what our civilized mythology tells us)? How do we define natural and unnatural? How do we define domestic? What causes domestication to begin with? Why would we want to rewild? Why would you want to undo domestication? What stands in the way of undoing domestication? How do we surpass these obstacles that prevent us from rewilding? Without fully understanding the answers to these questions, the term *rewilding* looks to most civilized people I've encountered like it simply means "getting back to nature" or "primitive living."

Rewilding refers to the action of participating in the social and economic renaissance of humans who use the preexisting social and economic models of our hunter-gatherer-gardener ancestors to recreate the sustainable relationship that humans had with their ecosystems and relatives for millions of years before the recent advent of agriculture, empire, and civilization. This critique emerged from modern ecological and anthropological studies that show how civilization, agriculture, and empire inherently destroy the landbase on which we depend for our survival.

Rather than trying to fix a model built on unstable ground, rewilding creates a new culture using an ancient recipe.

Rewilders recognize that as long as empire exists, it will force people into domestication and prevent rewilding from taking place. In order for rewilding to occur, empire must not exist. This reveals one of the complexities of rewilding in comparison with, say, the idea of "simple living" or "getting back to nature." The collapse and removal of empire stands as a pivotal topic in rewilding.

In order to accomplish rewilding, rewilders practice a multitude of skills such as innovative team building, storytelling, martial arts, and ancient hand crafts like braintanning deer skins into buckskins and making tools from stone, bone, and wood. Because rewilders see rewilding as part of a transition culture, they do not shun the use of modern technologies such as computers, guns, and cars, knowing that those technologies rely on an unsustainable industrial economy and will not last through the end of empire.

In order to create a holistic culture empathetic to the land and our other-than-human neighbors, rewilders emphasize storytelling and sensory exercises that provide experiences in animism. Animism, which lies at the heart of rewilding, refers to a way of seeing and experiencing the world and its other-than-human members as beings who demand respect and not inanimate objects put here for humans to exploit.

Creating and maintaining wild or feral cultures marks the goal of rewilding. Rewilding does not denote an end point but rather a continuing cultural process of learning how to relate to the land, people, and other-than-humans in a sustainable way. Even wild or feral cultures practice the art of rewilding.

After all this time, I've finally come up with a (rather
mechanistic) definition that I think will at least explain
a lot more to the average person, and perhaps pique their
interest and let them see rewilding through a more complex lens than the previous definition:

> **Rewild,** *verb*: to foster and maintain a sustain-
> able way of life through hunter-gatherer-gardener
> social and economic systems, including but not
> limited to the encouragement of social, physical,
> spiritual, mental, and environmental biodiversity
> and the prevention and undoing of social, physical,
> spiritual, mental, and environmental domestica-
> tion and enslavement

Domestication vs. Rewilding

How do we define *wild*? We now know that "wild" hunter-gatherer cultures greatly manipulated their environments. Where do we draw the line between *wild* and *domestic*? Rewilding means undoing domestication. If we wish to understand what that fully entails, we must examine the words *wild*, *natural*, *unnatural*, and *domestic* as we have come to know them in the context of civilization.

Domestic comes from the Latin *domesticus*, meaning "belonging to the household." Domesticates belong to the household. We could interpret this in many ways, depending on our own personal perception of "the household." If we perceive the whole world as a house that we all (humans and other-than-humans) belong to, I see no problem with the term *domestic*. Culturally, however, we know that civilization does not define the word in those terms, but in terms of belonging to the house of humans. After all, the word has an uncle, *dominion*, which god told us in Genesis we hold over all things natural. *Dominion* comes from the Latin *dominionem*, "ownership." Let's not forget *dominion*'s nephew, *domination*, which means "to rule or have dominion over." Or, if we think back to the terms of a "house," it means "lord, master of the house." *Domestic* refers to all forms of creation that we (civilization) master over.

The term *master*, as opposed to *collaborator*, demonstrates the basic differences between wild and domestic relationships: control. The difference between a wild and free, commensal symbiotic relationship and a domestic, parasitic one involves the commitment to control or the will to have power *over* rather than share power *with*.

In *The Culture of Make Believe*, Derrick Jensen defines *natural* and *unnatural* in this way:

> Any ritual, artifact, process, action is natural to the degree that it reinforces our understanding of our embeddedness in the natural world, and any ritual, artifact, process, action is unnatural to the degree that it does not.

If every living creature has a connection to those it consumes and those who consume it, the genetics of both will affect both. Domestication removes all variables concerning the life and genetic changes of an organism. When we do not allow other animals to eat plants (through fences, "pest" control, etc.), we remove a variable of genetic strength. When we breed animals and plants for genetic traits based on living in an entirely human-manipulated environment, we remove the variables of dynamic environments and they lose genetic strength in the real world. Over time this makes them dependent on human culture (specifically agriculture, factory farming, and civilization). It also feels like a lot of work for the controller (constant weeding, tilling, fertilizing, genetic engineering). Domestication ignores our embeddedness in the natural world and seeks to control it. Using the above definition of *natural* and *unnatural*, we can refer to the process of domestication as unnatural.

Controller or controlled, both species breed weakness into their genes, and in our case culture. Put a civilized human in the "wild" (which to domestic peoples means "anywhere outside our control"), and they will have a very difficult time meeting their most basic needs. We have become so dependent on domesticated species that we have physically and culturally domesticated ourselves.

A natural relationship breeds mutually beneficial relationships that build strength in a given and changing environment with variables outside of human control. As greater environments change through shifts in climate and other environmental factors, these relationships maintain a fluctuating baseline. Civilized people believe that in nature you must "eat others or find yourself eaten." Yet the reality of nature suggests that you must caretake the things you eat, or you will die. If five species eat salmon, all five of those species must caretake the salmon. If one species caretakes wheat (and prevents anyone else from eating it), the web of support breaks and both wheat and wheat eater become weak. With many life forms tending each other, if one species chain breaks, the other species will not feel as stressed, since many others tend to them.

Rewilding means returning to a more natural or wild state and reversing domestication. It means increasing our commensal symbiotic relationships with humans, and more importantly with other-than-humans. This doesn't mean we just "let things grow." Commensal symbiotic relationships do not mean "hands off!" It means learning to tend the lives of those we eat, so that they keep on living and so do we.

Agriculture vs. Rewilding

In order to understand the destructive nature of agriculture, you must understand the phases of ecological succession. Ecological succession refers to the phases of growth from barren rock to a climax forest. The loss of biodiversity that creates a blank slate generally occurs through a disturbance such as fire, flood, or volcanic eruption.

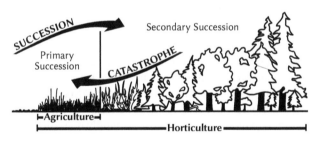

Figure 1: Ecological succession and subsistence strategies

Primary succession refers to the earliest phase of ecological succession, characterized by the growth of pioneer plants such as fungi, grasses, and annual wildflowers. These plants love sun, barren rock and/or disturbed soil, and serve to create quality, life-giving soil that makes secondary succession possible. Secondary succession refers to the later phases of ecological succession, marked by the growth of larger perennials such as shrubs and trees, which need established soil. These phases work towards creating the final stage of succession, a stable ecosystem, referred to as a climax forest.

Agriculture refers to a process of cultivation that simulates natural catastrophe (such as burning, flooding, tilling) to inspire annual pioneer plants, specifically grasses like corn, wheat, and rice. From its foundation, agriculture causes a loss of biodiversity. Agricultural subsistence means keeping the land in a fixed state of primary succession. Agriculturalists have a fondness for monocropping. Monocropping sets up the perfect environment for insects who love to eat that particular plant. Slowly but surely, tilling to create continuous primary succession exposes the soil to wind and rain until it erodes away entirely—so much so that in order to grow crops, fields require the importation of mineral resources known as fertilizer.

Ecological succession shows us that plant growth naturally progresses to climax forests. Agriculture works against, rather than with, this natural progression. Trying to stop insect populations when you have provided them the perfect habitat requires a lot of work. Making fertilizers that you would not need if you followed the flow of succession requires a lot of work. Not only does this form of subsistence destroy the environment, it also requires a massive amount of labor (which characteristically comes in the form of a slave class).

Agriculture creates an extreme vulnerability to crop failure from large insect infestations, disease, and climate change. This inevitably leads to famine. If you put all your eggs in the agriculture basket, you die. In order to combat this, agriculturalists invented food storage, aka the granary. Initially this looks great—a little more work on their part, but in the end they don't starve to death during crop failures. Unfortunately, food surplus affects the population growth of a species inspiring it to grow.

Any animal population with a surplus of food grows to match that surplus, humans included. A population cannot grow without an increase in food availability, usually through an increase in "efficiency" in food production. Therefore a population explosion implies more food production. Full-time agriculturalists with a food surplus create a positive feedback loop of growing more food to feed an ever-expanding population. Eventually the soil beneath them degrades and washes away, and they cease practicing agriculture, as we have seen with many civilizations; or as in the case of our civilization, they expand into neighboring forests and keep growing.

Civilization, a way of life characterized by the growth of cities, works as an ecological phenomenon occurring when agricultural peoples reach a certain population density due to their food-surplus-induced population growth positive feedback loop. Though not a catastrophe in the "natural" sense, as in fires, floods, volcanic eruptions, and comets, in ecological terms you can literally call civilization a catastrophe. Perhaps "cultural catastrophe" would serve as the best description.

It feels worth noting that many First Nations peoples and other indigenous peoples around the world heavily cultivated the lands they lived with in a manner very different from agriculture. These methods have many names, but I prefer the term *horticulture*.

Horticulture refers to cultivation by means of secondary succession: perennial shrubs and trees, aka forests. This still involves burning, selective harvesting, crop rotation, pruning, transplanting, minor tilling, and weeding. These methods can also lead to population growth, but they do not lead to overall loss of biodiversity and soil as agriculture does. This also does not mean to say that horticulturalists never used agricultural practices, but that agricultural foods never formed a staple of their diet.

Many people have a difficult time understanding the differences between horticulture and agriculture. This may occur because some agricultural strategies cross over into horticultural strategies. Linguistically the term *agriculture* comes from the Latin *agri* (field) and *cultura* (cultivation). *Horticulture* combines *hortus* (garden) and *cultura*. Cultivating a field versus cultivating a garden. We can see the implications of agriculture's monocropping primary succession plant obsession in its very name. We can also understand the implications of horticulture's diversity of plants and smaller-scale style through its name.

We can distinguish between the two by observing the results of how the strategy affects the land. Does it create more biodiversity or less? Does it strengthen the biological community or weaken it? It seems like a good idea to create a list of horticultural and agricultural strategies and reveal how and why you can use them to create more life, or misuse them to create less.

Agriculture uses strategies of cultivation such as transplanting, seeding, tilling, burning, pruning, fertilizing, selective harvesting, crop rotation, and so on. But the main difference between agriculture and horticulture involves agriculture's focus on using these tools to create one habitat: meadow or field. Horticulture uses the same strategies of cultivation to promote ecological succession and diversity of landscapes. Let's go through and find out for ourselves.

Catastrophe: burning vs. tilling

When I hear the word *tilling*, the classic image of a farmer and his plow pops into my head. I can see the deep trenches the plow has cut into the land in pretty rows. I can smell the sweetness of the upturned earth. Tilling works as an artificial catastrophe. Burning also works as a catastrophe. Frequent small-scale burns return nutrients to the soil without killing the roots of desired species. Burning also eliminates succession and prevents large-scale fires from occurring.

Soil aeration: sticks vs. steel

Gophers and moles dig holes and aerate the soil. Foragers use digging sticks to forage roots, tubers, and rhizomes. This breaks up the earth, making it easier for the roots to grow, and aerates the soil. The plow, on the other hand, goes too deep and destroys the mycorrhizal network of fungi that distributes nutrients to plants. It also aerates the soil, but it goes too deep and causes the soil to dry too much, which leads to soil loss and erosion.

Irrigation: sticks vs. stone

Beavers build small-scale dams with sticks that create flood plains, wetlands, and marshes that provide habitat for aquatic life. Humans too have replicated this on a small scale. Civilization builds insanely large dams of stone that destroy the river's life by draining too much water and drying it out.

Seeding

Any squirrel will tell you, if you want to ensure that you have more to eat year after year, plant a few more seeds than you'll dig up to eat during the winter.

Transplanting

Transplanting looks the same as seeding to me. Do you consider a seed a plant? What about seeds that germinate into plants and then grow through rhizome? Some willow trees can lose a branch, only to have that branch drift downstream and grow into a whole new plant! Wait, would you consider it new if it came from a preexisting tree? Do they share the same soul? Have I gone too deep for a chapter about horticulture and agriculture?

Fertilizing: poop vs. petrol

Shit. We all do it. Poop turns into fertilizer. Controlled burns also work as fertilizer by quickly breaking down dead wood and making their nutrients bio-available. Agriculturalists just import nutrients from other areas, and in the case of oil, from under the ground.

Pesticides

Foragers and horticulturalists also used burning to keep down insect populations. Civilization uses toxic chemicals that poison not only bugs but also the soil, the water, the birds, and our own bodies.

Pruning and coppicing

Beaver pruning stimulates willows, cottonwood, and aspen to regrow bushier the next spring. Black bears break branches. Hunter-gatherers prune trees too, to encourage larger yields and materials for making tools like baskets.

Monocropping

Horticulturalists don't use this technique, which exists uniquely to agriculturalists. Probably the larger symptom of control and domestication. No weeds in my field!

Selective harvesting: strength vs. weakness

Every animal uses this technique. Wolves thin out the sick and weak deer. Sometimes you take the weak so the strong survive. Sometimes you eat the strong so your poop will fertilize the seed. Selective harvesting shows us that systems evolve to work in cooperation. If we look closely we can see the outcome of our decisions. Domestication also works as a form of selective harvesting, only rather than strengthening the plant or animal, it weakens it. I go more into this aspect in "Domestication vs. Rewilding."

Seasonal rotation

Aside from building strength through selective harvesting, seasonal rotation of lands and food sources, and even yearly rotations, allow an area to restore itself from the temporary impacts of the harvest.

Many people also make the assumption that those who practice horticulture long enough eventually begin to practice agriculture. I'd like to suggest that this perceived continuum from foraging to agriculture does not exist. I'd like to suggest that a continuum between foragers and horticultural peoples exists, but agriculture appears as a completely different beast. It works *in opposition to* the fundamental restorative principles that shape the continuum between foraging and horticulture. Although it uses mostly intensified horticultural practices, it disregards the most basic ecological principles.

Foragers, hunter-gatherers, and horticulturalists used (and in some places, continue to use) the aforementioned methods to build soil and create varying habitats of succession, creating more ecotones and increasing biodiversity. If a continuum existed, we would see a decrease in biodiversity in each new phase of the continuum: hunter-gatherers would decrease biodiversity more than foragers, and horticulturalists would decrease biodiversity more than hunter-gatherers. Because we don't see this, we can guess that agriculture exists outside of that subsistence continuum as a completely different beast.

Many people use the term *agriculture* too loosely. Expressions like *sustainable agriculture* make no sense when you take into account the origin of the word *agriculture*. *Sustainable agriculture* looks like an oxymoron. We need to differentiate between agriculture (the field or monocrop) and horticulture (the garden of forest succession) if we want to live sustainably.

This doesn't mean that everything labeled "horticulture" falls under a sustainable practice. On the contrary, most fruit-bearing trees these days come in the form of clones—one plant spliced onto the rootstock of a similar plant and pruned to encourage the graft, a perfect clone of the original. Generally these plants have no fertility on their own, which means they rely completely on their human caretakers. I can't think of a worse fate nor a better example of domestication.

To take the next step, we must translate this knowledge into practical use. The question presses: How can we change our subsistence strategies from agriculturing supermarkets to horticulturing-hunting-gathering villages? How can we go from stupid-civilized-urban-dweller to hotshot-rewilding-horticultural-hunter-gatherer?

Keep reading.

At the core of rewilding lies the dismantling and abandonment of agricultural subsistence, a catastrophic practice to which we all act as slaves. We must create a new way of life using such ancient techniques as horticulture and its modern cousin, permaculture, as a transition to or to supplement a hunter-gatherer lifestyle.

Generalization vs. Rewilding

We know that humans who lived here for millions of years did so in a sustainable fashion. We know that civilization has caused one of the largest mass extinctions in only a few thousand. We know that the thousands of cultures that did not practice agriculture and create civilizations lived in a sustainable way. We know that a lot of those cultures had cultural contamination by contact with civilization by the time anthropologists wrote about them. Fortunately, enough writing on less-touched cultures exists so that we can estimate how much civilization contaminated an indigenous culture before anthropologists wrote about them. For example, when someone argues that rape and spousal abuse existed in indigenous cultures, we can often link that behavior to post-contact with civilization. I don't mean to say that all hunter-gatherers had a perfect life. Assuredly not. Humans, after all, belong to the animal kingdom, and environmental pressures can cause any number of conflicts.

Respecting indigenous traditions and mindful of cultural appropriation, I approach these cultures from a systems perspective, without fixating on their particular dogmas or ceremonies. I generalize because I speak of the overwhelming similarities in their respective systems approaches to participating with the land and each other. I generalize because the evidence says I can. Any exception

usually reflects some form of contamination by civilization (as in the example of rape) or a cultural difference
(like group sex, circumcision, warfare) that has nothing
to do with the principles behind rewilding, only working
as a straw man to keep the fundamental unsustainability
of civilization from coming to light. If you have trouble
understanding this, please read some modern anthropol-
ogy.

This all means to say that when I talk about horticulturalists, hunter-gatherers, indigenous peoples, primitive
peoples, native cultures, wild peoples, or animist cultures,
I generally mean those cultures that lived for millions of
years in a sustainable way and had little to no contamination from civilized culture. When I use words like agriculture, agriculturalists, civilizationists, civilized, domestic,
or domesticated, I refer to the current culture that does
not live in a sustainable or desirable way.

Appropriation vs. Rewilding

A few (always white) people have attacked me as a cultural appropriator. If I learned a Lakota song, recorded it, and sold it to others, you could call me a cultural appropriator. If I make a fire using a bow-drill, that doesn't count as appropriation, because it represents a piece of technology widely distributed around the world and carries no dogmatic cultural practice with it. I don't benefit financially from the sale of particular indigenous traditional cultural practices. You won't see me sell a line of traditional Chanupa pipes.

If I made a traditional Northwest Coast mask, in that particular artistic style, that would look like cultural appropriation. But I will talk about how the Northwest Coast cultures encourage biodiversity through their perception of, and practices with, the land. I will talk about how we can restore this relationship in our own way using the same practices. You cannot call that appropriation.

Many indigenous authors and teachers have explained that no one owns these skills. Now, that doesn't mean I practice particular, long-standing traditions of a particular indigenous people (such as the potlatch), but that I study their systems, and the systems of my own ancestors, and create my own using the same principles.

For example, my friend Brian and I led a sweat lodge at a

summer camp. That does not count as cultural appropriation because we didn't use any particular native culture
songs or themes. Cultures from around the world use
sweat lodges. You sit in a little room with hot rocks in
the middle and pour water on them. We also call it a
steam bath. The basic principle here involves sweating
out toxins to cleanse yourself. Now if you dress it with
Lakota songs, and have no Lakota ancestry, that works as
appropriation. If you make up your own songs or sing the
songs of your own culture (I like Cat Stevens' *If You Want
to Sing Out*), you have started to rewild.

This subject evokes a lot of emotion in many parties.
Cultural appropriation has really destroyed and further
disrespected indigenous cultures affected by civilization.
Rewilding does not mean appropriating native cultures. It
means helping them thrive again, as we help ourselves to
do the same. We all have native ancestry if we trace back
far enough. Rewilding means respectfully learning from
our hunter-gatherer ancestors as well as from those alive
today, honoring their long-standing traditions so that we
can reestablish a sustainable relationship with the land
that benefits all generations of life to come.

Civilization vs. Rewilding

You might assume that writing a chapter called "Civilization vs. Rewilding" would come easy since civilization means the exact opposite of rewilding. Then I got to thinking: *most people don't know what civilization means.*

American Heritage Dictionary defines civilization thusly:

1. An advanced state of intellectual, cultural, and material development in human society, marked by progress in the arts and sciences, the extensive use of record-keeping, including writing, and the appearance of complex political and social institutions

2. The type of culture and society developed by a particular nation or region or in a particular epoch: *Mayan civilization; the civilization of ancient Rome*

3. The act or process of civilizing or reaching a civilized state

4. Cultural or intellectual refinement; good taste

5. Modern society with its conveniences: *returned to civilization after camping in the mountains*

These definitions reek of a culture with a superiority complex. I love how the line "the appearance of complex political and social institutions" sounds like a glossed-over way of saying *slavery*. In order to fully grasp what civilization means, let's go on a little definition journey. The first path we take will lead us to redefine many of the words commonly found among mythologists and anthropologists. As we explore these concepts, they will become tools, not static objects. Take this definition of a hammer:

> A hand tool that has a handle with a perpendicularly attached head of metal or other heavy rigid material, and is used for striking or pounding

Notice how the definition describes what makes a hammer: a handle with a perpendicularly attached head of metal or other heavy rigid material. Notice also that this definition includes the use of a hammer: striking or pounding. This shows us an example of a dynamic definition. Most of the words I use do not include usage in their definitions. The more we begin to perceive them as tools for rewilding, the greater the need to include their purpose or use, within their definition. So that we can communicate on the same page, we'll start by redefining and refining definitions of words in the vocabulary of those-who-rewild.

Okay, this may sound strange, but let's start with *art*. How do we define this word? *American Heritage Dictionary* gives me this definition:

1. Human effort to imitate, supplement, alter, or counteract the work of nature

2. a. The conscious production or arrangement of sounds, colors, forms, movements, or other elements in a manner that affects the sense of beauty, specifically the production of the beautiful in a graphic or plastic medium

   b. The study of these activities

    c. The product of these activities; human works of beauty considered as a group

These definitions describe art physically but leave us with no understanding of why. Why do humans produce conscious arrangement of sounds, colors, forms, movements? Why do humans make stuff? Something as seemingly instinctual as art must have a purpose. Humans have a complex language and live as storytellers; art gives us a way of telling a story. Whether we use one image or a thousand, a piece of art contains a story. So the purpose of making art works to tell a story. Maybe we don't see this in the dictionary because it serves a subconscious function? Regardless, this leads to another question: why do we tell stories?

Story, *noun*:

1. An account or recital of an event or a series of events, either true or fictitious, as:

    a. An account or report regarding the facts of an event or group of events: *The witness changed her story under questioning*

    b. An anecdote: *came back from the trip with some good stories*

    c. A lie: *told us a story about the dog eating the cookies*

2. a. A usually fictional prose or verse narrative intended to interest or amuse the hearer or reader; a tale

    b. A short story

3. The plot of a narrative or dramatic work

4. A news article or broadcast

5. Something viewed as or providing material for a literary or journalistic treatment: *"He was*

> *colorful, he was charismatic, he was controversial, he was a good story"* (Terry Ann Knopf)

6. The background information regarding something: *What's the story on these unpaid bills?*

7. Romantic legend or tradition: *a hero known to us in story*

Yeah, yeah. But why? We use a hammer for striking or pounding. What do we use story for? Why do we tell stories? I have asked many groups this question and have heard answers like, "So someone won't make the same mistakes," "So we can learn from the past." These don't satisfy me. Maybe we should look at where storytelling came from. The word *myth* has many connotations, mainly bad ones. Some people hear the word and equate it to a lie. Others conjure images of ancient Greek or Roman gods. When I use the word *myth* I mean something very different. In order to understand civilization and its functions, we need to give *myth* and how we perceive it a makeover. Let's take a look at the definition:

1. a. A traditional, typically ancient story dealing with supernatural beings, ancestors, or heroes that serves as a fundamental type in the worldview of a people, as by explaining aspects of the natural world or delineating the psychology, customs, or ideals of society: *the myth of Eros and Psyche; a creation myth*

   b. Such stories considered as a group: *the realm of myth*

2. A popular belief or story that has become associated with a person, institution, or occurrence, especially one considered to illustrate a cultural ideal: *a star whose fame turned her into a myth; the pioneer myth of suburbia*

3. A fiction or half-truth, especially one that forms part of an ideology

4. A fictitious story, person, or thing: *"German artillery superiority on the Western Front was a myth" (Leon Wolff)*

Did you notice they made no mention of what people use myths for? I did. Three definitions above say that a myth means a story. Three include ideology. Let's redefine a myth as a story that holds a culture's ideology. So then, what purpose do we have in telling a story that holds a cultural ideology? In *The Power of Myth*, Joseph Campbell said,

> The ancient myths were designed to harmonize the mind and the body. The mind can ramble off in strange ways and want things that the body does not want. The myths and rites were a means of putting the mind in accord with the body, and the way of life in accord with the way nature dictates.

If ancient myths mean to put the human way of life in accord with the way nature dictates, how do we know "the way nature dictates?" If that shows us the purpose of the ancient myths, what of the purpose of current myths? Do we have a general purpose of mythology that spans both ancient and current?

Culture:

a. The totality of socially transmitted behavior patterns, arts, beliefs, institutions, and all other products of human work and thought

b. These patterns, traits, and products considered as the expression of a particular period, class, community, or population: *Edwardian culture*; *Japanese culture*; *the culture of poverty*

c. These patterns, traits, and products considered
with respect to a particular category, such as a
field, subject, or mode of expression: *religious
culture in the Middle Ages*; *musical culture*; *oral
culture*

d. The predominating attitudes and behavior that
characterize the functioning of a group or organization

Again, no description of the purpose or use or function
of culture. To learn the purpose of an opposable thumb,
you would study the physical evolution of the human.
Similarly, to understand the purpose of culture you must
study the social evolution of humans. In the preface to
Iron John, Robert Bly writes:

> The knowledge of how to build a nest in a bare tree,
> how to fly to the wintering place, how to perform
> the mating dance — all of this information is stored
> in the reservoirs of the bird's instinctual brain. But
> human beings, sensing how much flexibility they
> might need in meeting new situations, decided to
> store this sort of knowledge outside the instinctual
> system; they stored it in stories.

If you have ever gone out animal tracking you'll find it
easy to see how the human brain developed. The brain
takes in information from the senses, links it together, and
forms a story. Say you come across a set of footprints
on the ground. You can consider a million things when
reading it. Who made it? When? Where did they plan to
go? Consider the terrain. A track in the sand ages completely differently from one in mud, clay, snow, debris, or
grass. Once you have considered the terrain, you must
think about weather. Has it felt sunny? Rainy? Windy?
All these factors age the track in different ways, and of

course, each terrain acts differently too. Each animal's track ages differently depending on weather and terrain. How can you tell that seven days and three hours ago a hungry fox traveled east in a hunting-style trot? And what other information will this tell you about the local environment? Does the fox hunt here often? If so, what does that tell you about the environment?

To get to the root of what it means to live as humans, we must look at this question: what happened here? This question separates us from other animals. We have the ability to question and tell stories in a way other animals don't. Other animals tell each other stories too, though. A wolf out on a scout mission finds something interesting. It rubs its body onto the scent and travels back to the pack where they greet it and smell it. The wolf has carried this story in the form of a scent. The scent can only tell the wolves what lies there, but it cannot give them any more insight into the ecology or awareness beyond their senses. This shows us where humans function differently. We evolved to ask, "What happened here?" We can carry the story beyond the moment. The second part of tracking requires the ability to communicate the story to others in order to lead us to shelter, water, fire, and food. The better the storyteller, the better the chance of survival. Tracking works as the art of questioning and the telling of the story. Like the hammer, storytelling functions as a survival tool.

Human culture formed by two simultaneous evolutionary transformations. The formation of a social organization reveals the first transformation. Animals evolve into social organizations because cooperation proves advantageous for the group of cooperators as a whole. Therefore the purpose of culture becomes obvious: ease of survival. Robert Bly hinted at the second process: the externalization of instinctual survival into stories or myths. So you could say that language, art, storytelling, and myths all function as a means of survival. But wait. Because every culture differs and varies in survival ideology, myth would not function as a means for human survival as a species but for a specific culture. This means that a myth works as a story that holds a specific culture's ideology for the purpose of survival. These ideologies serve as blueprints for a culture, coming to life through mythological enactment or ritual.

Ritual:

1. a. The prescribed order of a religious cere-mony
   b. The body of ceremonies or rites used in a place of worship

2. a. The prescribed form of conducting a for-mal secular ceremony: *the ritual of an in-auguration*
   b. The body of ceremonies used by a fraternal organization

3. A book of rites or ceremonial forms

4. Rituals:

   a. A ceremonial act or a series of such acts
   b. The performance of such acts

5. a. A detailed method of procedure faithfully or regularly followed: *My household chores have become a morning ritual*
   b. A state or condition characterized by the presence of established procedure or rou-tine: *"Prison was a ritual reenacted daily, year in, year out. Prisoners came and went; generations came and went; and yet the rit-ual endured" (William H. Hallahan)*

Because myths hold a "detailed method" of survival, we find ourselves instinctually programmed to "faithfully or regularly" follow them. When humans make choices, they enact the mythology of their culture. This means that every choice we make works as a ritual, and that ritual, again, serves as a function of survival. This brings up a discussion of free will and whether such a thing really exists. If all our choices come conditioned by a mythology, we make no choices without external influence. I watched a movie about fast cars. I made the unconscious choice to drive fast. I had enough awareness to consciously realize this and choose to slow down because of another mythology called Johnny Law. Both choices I made came from mythology: the story of fun (driving fast) and the story of consequence (getting a ticket).

Culture means more than just "the totality of socially transmitted behavior patterns." It refers to a working system of two parts: mythology and ritual. Kept alive by transmitting its survival ideologies through mythology. This transmission leads to ritual enactment. Cyclical ideals and actions.

My definitions thus far:

> **Mythology:** A story that holds cultural ideology
> for the purpose of survival
>
> **Ritual:** Choices made for the purpose of survival
>
> **Culture:** Socially organized humans enacting an
> ideology for the purpose of survival

But now we have a problem. To define a myth as story that contains survival ideology would mean to ignore that all stories contain fragments of a culture's survival ideology. All stories would appear as myths. Since all art works as a form of telling a story, and considering that all human interaction means telling stories, you could define a myth as "human communication." But this dilutes the definition quite a bit now. How about that word *meme*?

> **Meme:** A unit of cultural information, such as a cultural practice or idea, that we transmit verbally or by repeated action from one mind to another

I hate this word. Many people do. It works as an analogy to *gene* but does not mimic the genetic process in any other way. Many people argue this and spend their waking hours taking it to the extreme trying to match it perfectly. But mostly I hate how dry it feels, how scientific it sounds. Not to mention the way it avoids delineating action from idea. I hate the word *meme* and don't use it. I just wanted to let you know that people have used these other words, *myth* and *ritual*, to describe memes for a long, long time, and *meme* appears useless, just a cool analogy to *gene*. But for all you memetic freaks out there, this just shows another way of looking at it. Let's break down the definition of *meme*: a unit of cultural information, such as a cultural practice or idea (ideologies or worldview), that we transmit verbally (story) or by repeated action (ritual) from one mind to another.

So where do myths come from? How do we form them? In *The Power of Myth*, Joseph Campbell and Bill Moyers discuss how myths come from people responding to their environment. Because myths form a detailed method of survival, I think we can take this one step further and say that myths (or memes) come from a culture's relationship to the environment. The way a culture interacts with its environment. It makes sense to say that ancient survival ideologies evolved to work in accord with "the way nature dictates," or we wouldn't stand here today.

In *Never Cry Wolf*, Farley Mowat discovered a connection
between the wolves' hunting style and the health of the
deer population. He found that wolves only hunt the
sick or weak members of a herd. This promotes healthy
genetics for the deer herds, which in turn benefits the
wolves by providing a constant food supply. They give
back to the deer by the method in which they kill them.
The better an animal can fit into its environment, the more
success it will have, as will the health of the entire ecosystem. Author Derrick Jensen calls this "survival of the fit."
Joseph Campbell called it "the way nature dictates." Farley
Mowat (and later Daniel Quinn) called it "The Law of Life."

In other animals we call this behavior instinct. The instinctual knowledge of "how human culture fits into the
environment" describes what we originally exported into
story. Humans mythologized this relationship and understanding into a worldwide religion known as animism.
Anthropologists of our culture studying indigenous cultures throughout the world coined the term. It appeared
as though every indigenous culture they came across in
their studies believed the following:

Animism:

1. The belief in the existence of individual spirits
   that inhabit natural objects and phenomena
2. The belief in the existence of spiritual beings
   that are separable or separate from bodies
3. The hypothesis holding that an immaterial
   force animates the universe

Coined hundreds of years ago by pretentious, culture-
eating anthropologists, no doubt this definition appears
very superficial. It lacks an understanding of the relationship to the environment that created the belief system

to begin with. It lacks purpose and function. Animism serves cultures by giving them instructions for living in accord with their environments.

Looking at this definition of culture, we can see an inherent weakness. If the story becomes damaged and loses sight of "the way nature dictates," the culture and land suffer. How does civilization's story differ from animism? How does civilization relate to the environment, in contrast to hunter-gatherers?

Let's look again at how good ol' *American Heritage* defines it:

Civilization:

1. An advanced state of intellectual, cultural, and material development in human society, marked by progress in the arts and sciences, the extensive use of record-keeping, including writing, and the appearance of complex political and social institutions

2. The type of culture and society developed by a particular nation or region or in a particular epoch: *Mayan civilization; the civilization of ancient Rome*

3. The act or process of civilizing or reaching a civilized state

4. Cultural or intellectual refinement; good taste

5. Modern society with its conveniences: *returned to civilization after camping in the mountains*

Of course, conquerors write history. "An advanced state of intellectual...blah, blah, blah." No one ever looks at what makes all this backslapping and high-fiving possible: the devouring of the world. The conquerors spend so much time thinking so highly of themselves they have little time to notice how they fuck up ecosystems. Civilization does not listen to "the way nature dictates" at all. In fact, in order to support these "advanced" systems, they not only ignore nature but actually foster a hatred of the natural world. If we look at all previous civilizations, we know that full-time agriculture gave rise to their runaway population growth, and ultimately their death as the soil eroded beneath them. I define civilization thusly:

> A catastrophe created when a human culture practices full-time agriculture, causing their populations to spiral into a cycle of exponential growth, social hierarchy, soil depletion, and genocidal expansion that leads to an eventual collapse of ecosystems, biological diversity, and culture

Indigenous peoples did (and still do) not live in a culture of civilization because they did not practice full-time agriculture, nor grow to live in such density that they required imported, agriculturally produced grains from a distant country. I hate it so much when I say, "Native peoples didn't have a civilization," and a civilized drone says, "Yes they did! Your comment sounds so racist! They did too have a civilization, it just looked different from ours!" I have to calmly say, "Eh hem. You have no fucking idea what civilization means. They had complex cultures, sure. Sustainable, beautiful cultures that worked *better than civilization*." I call these *cultures*. And yes, they had art and music and language and fashion and everything civilization tries to claim a monopoly on. But they didn't build *cities*.

Civilization continues because its cultural blueprints (mythos) and infrastructure (ritual propagation of dams, tanks, buildings, soldiers, consumers, etc.) go unchallenged, even in the face of collapse. It exists in the

ethereal realm of mythology and manifests itself in the
physical through monocropped fields, concrete buildings,
bulldozers, and million-men armies. Rewilding presents
us with a challenge to civilized mythology, providing us
with a new set of cultural blueprints based on the ancient,
sustainable ones, and in full recognition of civilization's
inherent unsustainability.

Empire vs. Rewilding

A power system sits in place that keeps the rich richer and the poor poorer. This power system lies outside most people's perception because we grow up in it, never knowing anything different, never seeing it articulated, but understanding it down to our bones. It feels as natural to us as drinking a glass of water. This power structure keeps us as slaves, forced to continue building civilization. Without empire, civilization could not, would not, exist.

For a long time now I've focused myself more with the sustainable living aspect of rewilding and not so much with the social structures. But with all the green technology talk I've begun to worry. Even though ecologically it could never happen, let's pretend for a moment that civilization became sustainable. Sure, that might feel great *environmentally*, but what would that really mean for us *socially*?

Before the rise of cities that gave us the term *civilization*, empire and slavery existed. In fact, I would say that cities and civilization would not have come about without empire (rich elite with an army fueled by grain production) forcing people (slaves) to build them. What does empire mean, really, but a hierarchical social structure of masters with an army to force other humans into slavery? When people advocate for a "sustainable civilization," they don't realize that means they simultaneously advocate for the continuation of slavery.

A slave means someone forced into labor under the threat of death, torture, or some other form of abusive violence. It probably started kind of like this: a sedentary agricultural community had a population explosion. Something happened here. They went to their neighbors and said something like, "Give us 10% of your food or we will kill you." Several thousand years went by, and now we have taxes, rent, food bills, water bills, health insurance bills, electricity bills, gas bills, etc. All of which everyone pays for without question: "Well, of course you have to pay taxes!" We take in our slavery as we take in the air. Once a system like this gets going it becomes very hard to stop. If you say no, they have the power to kill you and steal your land. With an ever-growing population from grain-based agriculture, they will quickly fill your land with their ever-growing population of farmer slaves. If you say yes, you get assimilated and enslaved. If you run, you will have conflict with your neighbors, and if the expansion continues it will eventually reach you anyway.

Growing up as an American, I received a flawed, inborn understanding of how the rest of the world works. I grew up here, with electricity twenty-four hours a day, seven days a week. I grew up with television, telephones, and sports cars. I grew up with McDonalds, the Gap, Hot Topic, and so forth. With democracy, free speech, freedom of religion. My point: although we live as wage slaves and slaves to this culture, we live in the richest country in the world. Slaves...*with a lot of money.* Money in this instance translates to "rights." We have a lot of "rights" in America because we can afford to buy them from our masters (temporarily of course). This gives most Americans the illusion of the power of personal change through making the change in their own lives. They have the luxury (and delusion) of "buying green." They have the luxury of time and money to invest in their home permaculture gardens. Who else in the world has time or money or access to educational resources to do that? Maybe a few other first world countries, but not the majority of enslaved peoples.

I find it funny when I hear people say that our problems occur because people don't take personal responsibility. Blame the person, not the culture, not the system of wealth management and the armies that enforce it. Since climate change threatens us all, does that mean that a slave-child sewing soccer balls in Taiwan has a personal responsibility to stop climate change? Do you think the slaves in the third world have a personal responsibility to stop climate change? Do you honestly think they have the power? Where they can't even afford to buy "rights"? Do you honestly think us more privileged Americans do?

Of course, when most people I know speak of personal responsibility, their words carry an unspoken premise that means they *don't* try to stop corporations from creating fucked-up products and forcing people to buy them, but instead figure out ways in which they can learn to live without the fucked-up products or buy expensive "green" products. This ignores the entire system of how empire exerts its power. I have the wealth to buy organic vegetables and free-range meats. Although I pay rent, I have enough time and money to plant a garden and build a humanure composting system. But what about your average American wage slaver with two jobs and a family to feed? They shop at Walmart because they can't afford anything else. The majority of people around the world cannot afford personal change, and those in power do not allow it anyway. Sure, they still have a responsibility to stop corporations and those in power from killing the land, because they live on this planet. But the idea of personal change making a difference comes from privileged people with money.

Since personal change requires money, it can't work because the masses can't afford it. It also takes accountability away from corporations and the military, police, and legal systems that protect them. Since those with money and power don't want to lose that money and power, they have no interest in changing this system.

The overwhelming majority of hunter-gatherers had egalitarian cultures. Sometimes they had hierarchical cultures, but without slavery—sometimes with what anthropologists have labeled as slavery, but not quite the same. Regardless, they had, and still have today where they have not experienced genocide, nonhierarchical social structures based on cooperation rather than competition.

In the wild, competition among plants and animals happens rarely, and usually only during times of scarcity. Within agricultural communities, we see wealth funneled away from the majority towards the few rich people. If you have to give 10% or more of your own food supply, 10% you had to toil in the soil for, your own food becomes scarce. If you destroy the soil using agriculture and ruin your landbase, of course you'll have scarce resources. This fear of constant scarcity leads to intense competition. If people have lived on earth for more than three million years (as the archeological record shows), we can assume that they have lived in a cooperative system for the most part, and that those who didn't, didn't stand the test of time. Even though civilizations seem to outcompete hunter-gatherers during their peak, they don't last in the long run.

A rather large emphasis sits on creating nonhierarchical social models in rewilding. As long as empire exists, civilization will persist because those who sit atop the pyramid will continue to enslave us. Because agriculture lies at the heart of civilization's destructiveness, and because empire only becomes possible through grain-fueled population growth, empire will never stop using agriculture. Even if everyone went "green," empire would not, could not, stop destroying the *soil*. When people advocate for a sustainable civilization (which cannot exist), they generally don't realize that means they simultaneously advocate for the continuation of empire, of slavery. This happens because they haven't ever articulated what civilization actually means, nor how civilizations function ecologically or socially. It seems safe to assume that if someone talks about sustainability without talking about dismantling civilization and rewilding, they haven't made this articulation either.

We cannot rewild as long as empire exists. Those in power will continue destroying the world whether we help them or not, and they will continue to do so backed by million-men armies (and soon robot armies—seriously, youtube that shit), nuclear weapons, and a brain-washed slave class. The end of empire will happen whether or not we encourage its end. When the oil runs out, when the soil turns to salt, we will see the end of empire. Unfortunately we will also see the end of countless species, including possibly our own. We must do what we can to dismantle empire if we wish to rewild, if we wish to save some semblance of life here on this planet.

English vs. Rewilding

Modern English language quite literally comes from no place. No indigenous people spoke or speak it. It works as a conglomeration of languages, a mishmash made for one purpose: trade. If languages provide us with a context with which to perceive the world, then English programs people to see the living world through the lens of exploitation: trees as dollar bills, animals as units of meat, humans as slaves. English tells us from the moment we utter our first word to our last that the world exists for one purpose: commerce.

By now you may have noticed something weird or different about my writing style that you can't quite put your finger on. I'll let you in on a little secret. I've written this book in E-Prime (or English Prime), a version of the English language that excludes the use of the verb "to be." You heard me right. I do not use *is, was, am, were, be, been, are,* or any of their contractions. Stop for a second and write a paragraph or two or three and see if you can write without using "to be." Pretty hard, huh? Now just think how hard it would feel to write a whole book in it!

E-Prime came about because some very clever scientists realized that B-English ("regular" English, which does not exclude "to be") creates a false projection of reality. The world constantly changes, and B-English interferes with this change by attempting to fix reality in stone. It seems only natural that a sedentary culture that resists change would eventually evolve a language that projects our perception of control into the natural world. We do it with the plow, and we do it with our words.

While doing who knows what kind of experiments, these nerds discovered that an electron, when measured with one instrument, appears as a wave and when measured with a different instrument appears as a particle. We have a problem here: in Aristotelian B-English, an electron cannot "be" both a particle and a wave, as surely as a table cannot also "be" a chair. He realized that by "be-ing," we label something as it "is," fixing it into an unchangeable object.

For example, I cannot simultaneously "be" both stupid and smart. But what happens when Person A observes with a set of instruments (Person A's senses) that I have intelligence, and Person B observes through a different set of instruments (Person B's senses) that I say idiotic things? Our linguistic world eats itself, and arguments ensue. "To be" prevents us from experiencing a shared reality—something we need in order to communicate in a sane way. If someone sees something differently from another, our language prevents us from acknowledging the other's point of view by limiting our perception to fixed states. For example, if I say "*Star Wars* is a shitty movie," and my friend says, "*Star Wars* is not a shitty movie!" We have no shared reality, for in our language, truth lies in only one of our statements, and we can forever argue these truths until one of us writes a book and has more authority than the other. If on the other hand I say, "I hated *Star Wars*," I state my opinion as observed through my own senses. I state a more accurate reality by not claiming that *Star Wars* "is" anything, as it could "be" anything to anyone. Similarly one could say, "I've seen Urban Scout act like an idiot before," while another person could say, "Man, Urban Scout has really made me think. I really appreciate him." We have two perceptions that do not contradict one another but that came about from different perspectives.

"To be" plays god. It attempts to chisel reality in stone and works as the backbone of the civilized paradigm. Of course it does: its birthplace lies in the land of economic commerce, not a biological community. English works to domesticate the world as much as tilling means to domesticate it. Every element of our culture urges for domestication, for slavery. If language shapes how we perceive the world, nothing stands more fundamental (aside from the practice of agriculture itself) to this process of domestication than our own language.

Some people believe that language marked the beginning of hierarchy and we should walk away from language as well. But where do you draw the line? At vocalization? Birds vocalize. Body language? Every animal uses body language. Every animal has a language. If I run from a bear it will chase me. If I stand my ground and avoid eye contact, I let the bear know I don't mean harm. The bear will huff and gruff and bluff to test my stance. Eventually the bear will walk away and let me go. This confrontation has a language to it. Peaceful confrontations do as well. Birds use songs, companion calls, and alarms to communicate, to emphasize their body language.

We know that indigenous peoples lived sustainably with beautiful, poetic spoken languages. We also know that no indigenous cultures used the verb "to be." Knowing that, and understanding what "to be" does to our perception of reality, it makes sense that the first step to rewilding the English language should involve eliminating Aristotle's mistake. Willem Larsen has taken this concept much further and created "E-Primitive," a version of E-Prime that stresses verb-based sentences (among many other changes). Most indigenous languages based themselves in verbs rather than nouns. This shows us their focus on a fluid, ever-changing perception of reality. Our noun-based sentence structure shows us another symptom of our fixed-reality language.

E-Prime hardly fixes English (pardon the pun!). But it greatly defangs it. It tears down many of the language's footholds on control and allows for a more chaotic, changeable paradigm to fall into place. The more I write in E-Prime the more I see how "is" takes control of the world and how fluid English can sound. Of course, I speak B-English and use it in most of my other writings. I also have no illusions that E-Prime could ever stop civilization from destroying the planet. Rather, E-Prime works as a means of reconnecting myself to the wild through language. It merely helps me to see the world through a more dynamic, accurate linguistic paradigm.

Stockpiling vs. Rewilding

Hey there Scout,

I am just wondering that, while you are honing your skills to be able to create new out of the aftermath of civilization while nature is still intact, what are your thoughts about what to gather from this world (i.e. ropes, tarps, rations, guns) to facilitate survival during whatever happens whenever it happens. haha the future is so wonderfully vague but extremely heavy if you have the proper amount of imagination and paranoia! also do you have a place to escape to, do you think this is necessary? a plan on how to get there undetected, other people to join? i am working on all of these problems right now but my energy and focus rise and fall like the sun and that quickly and if its a nice day outside you can guarantee i am not focusing on the warm weather clothing and wool blankets i will need stowed, mostly working on my tan (vitamin d), muscles and ability to become nature as to remain undetectable. but i know there are things that are extremely important that will insure that the people with the right intentions for nature and the universe can prevail and that we should have these at the ready just in case anything happens. its funny because i have gone to some "survival" website with lists about what to have, they will list "at least a half gallon of water per day per individual, which does not provide water for hygiene, so be sure to take breath mints and STRONG DEODORANT" seriously these people are worried about "hygiene" and its the Apocalypse?!?!? i guess if they weren't intending to survive on MRES, which are sure to putrefy their systems, they wouldn't smell so foul but come on, if you even wear deodorant right now i am pretty sure you have a special comet with your name on it hurling towards the earth this second.

I don't know how well to say thanks but keep exploring and sharing,

Jessica

Hey Jessica,

Thanks for your questions! (And I appreciate your sense of humor.) I'm sure you can imagine I get questions like these fairly often. What supplies should I have for the SHTF (shit-hits-the-fan) scenario? Unfortunately most people hate my response...because I'm not really one of the SHTF people...

> While you are honing your skills to be able to create new out of the aftermath of civilization while nature is still intact.

I'd like to say first and foremost that I don't think of myself as honing my skills to have the abilities to create new out of the aftermath of civilization; rather, I work on creating a new world to live in right now because I don't like this one. I would do this work even if I didn't think of civilization as collapsing. Which I'd also like to say, started a long time ago. If we see that civilization has already started collapsing, we can start to see that collapse does not happen overnight, but rather like a slow and ugly death.

What will it take for people to fight back against civilization's destruction of the planet? When the salmon no longer swim upriver to spawn? When the polar bears no longer walk through the snow? I like to think of the SHTF scenario in the same way. How do you define your personal "shit"? When the salmon go, does that represent the shit hitting the fan? When the ice caps melt? etc.

Collapse works as a process, not an event. We can mark its progress by larger events, but the process itself happens rather slowly and painfully, depending on your addictions to civilization. I don't mean to say that fucked-up events that happen as a result of collapse can't happen overnight. Obviously tipping points (bigger pieces of "shit") exist in various systems, like the economy and the environment, and can bring about quick changes.

> What are your thoughts about what to gather from this world (i.e. ropes, tarps, rations, guns) to facilitate survival during whatever happens whenever it happens.

I think that the stockpile mentality represents a short-term strategy. Even if you stockpiled food for seven years, at the end of the seven years you'd better have a stable food production system in place. Generally people who spend time stockpiling don't have a long-term plan, and if they do it involves seed saving for farming and domestication of animals. The stockpiling person doesn't make a long-term plan because they operate under the belief that civilization will *recover*. "Survival skills" in the end only keep you alive long enough for *rescue*. Stockpiling only keeps you alive through an overnight tipping point you think will end at some point. In a total collapse scenario, civilized economic recovery will not occur. Not to the extent people will believe it to. So when we look at supplies, we need to imagine what level of technology, economy, and so forth we will maintain after collapse.

A stockpile represents a (false) sense of security. People want to feel that they have their bases covered: "Once I get everything on this list, I can survive anything!" Unfortunately for those people, that looks like a delusion. In this culture we teach that monetary wealth and possessions give us security. In natural systems, however, which will take precedence in collapse, cooperative relationships form the best way to maintain long-term security.

Now I can hear you all saying, "Sure, sure, Scout, love your neighbor and all that...But, uh, what should we stockpile?" It seems no matter how many times I explain this to people, they *still* want me to give them a list of supplies. What ends up happening when I do this? People just get the list of stuff and think that when something terrible happens they'll survive without any effort. Let me say it again: nothing you can do or buy will make you completely safe and secure as collapse intensifies or during a SHTF event. Who knows? Yes, you can do things and buy items that will increase your chances, but only in the short term. You need a long-term plan, and by that I mean you need a long-term relationship with the land, its other-than-human companions, and with people you can consider family who also have this relationship with the land and its other-than-human companions.

> Also do you have a place to escape to, do you think this is necessary? A plan on how to get there undetected, other people to join?

A lot of people have different ideas about this. Some people say you need to hunker down and stay put, that staying in a familiar place should sit at the top of your priorities. Again, this plan of "staying put" can only really mean that you expect a cultural recovery to take place. If you didn't expect a recovery, you would want to stay on the move, because once you (or your group) stay in one place long enough you will deplete the resources you depend on for survival.

A more long-term strategy would involve getting to know multiple pieces of land and tending them on a seasonal circuit, the way our hunter-gatherer ancestors did. Then you won't have to "escape" from anywhere, because you'll live right where you need to. And then we come back to the idea that rewilding does not imply preparedness, but re-creating a culture that uses regenerative principles.

> But I know there are things that are extremely important that will insure that the people with the right intentions for nature and the universe can prevail and that we should have these at the ready just in case anything happens.

The important things that will ensure the existence of people with the intention of not fucking up the planet or fucking over anyone, have to do not with stockpiling products but with stockpiling quality relationships.

"Okay, okay! Geez, Scout, I get it. But...seriously, what should I put in my survival kit?" Oh, shit. Fine. I'll tell you what I've got in my survival backpack!...But only if you promise to shut up about it already.

1. Carving knife
2. Leatherman tool
3. Water purifier
4. Water bottle
5. 12×12 camo tarp

·

6. Matches (in a waterproof container)
7. Three lighters
8. 100-ft parachute cord (you'll probably want more)
9. Spool of fishing line
10. Allen wrench set
11. Small crescent wrench
12. Rain jacket
13. Rain leggings
14. Spices/salt
15. Collapsible saw
16. Mini hatchet
17. Medium-sized metal pot (for boiling water/cooking)
18. Mini sewing kit
19. Small waterproof notebook
20. Pens
21. Sleeping bag (in waterproof stuff sack)
22. Road/topo maps
23. Backpacking stove with one extra fuel container
24. Roll of plastic baggies
25. Small battery-free flashlight (the kind you shake to charge)
26. Small Maglite with extra batteries

I think that list covers it. I'd take everything out and catalog it, but then I'd have to fit it all back in again and that takes fucking forever. One of the things you will notice about my list: I don't have food rations. Why? Because I know enough edible wild plants. I also know how to kill enough game, assuming of course that any exist in a total enviro-collapse scenario! But again, you can see that my list has nonrenewable expendables. Once they break, if I can't fix them, I'll need to know how to make them. To know how to make them, I'll need to know what trees serve what purposes. In order to know where the trees live, I'll need to have a preexisting relationship with the land. Etc. etc. etc. So, yeah. That about sums it all up. Don't rely on the short-term stockpile mythology. Learn the lay of the land, learn the plants and animals, and become comfortable as part of that system. Join the community of life.

"Primitive" Skills vs. Rewilding

I have always used the term *primitive skills* to refer to the creation of things like handmade tools such as the bow and arrow, social systems such as tribal organizations, educational systems such as mentoring, body skills such as heightening senses, or rituals such as giving thanks to the landbase. After spending several days at Rabbitstick Rendezvous, the oldest primitive skills gathering in the country, I figured out why I get a funny feeling when I tell people that I practice "primitive skills."

The term *primitive* can come across as racist to indigenous peoples. Throughout history, civilizationists have used the term as an excuse to kill, murder, and destroy these cultures. They use it to mean "lesser than." Even though most people I know do not use the word in this racist way, because of its history I feel it necessary to refrain from using it. For lack of a better term, I use it occasionally for ease among people who wouldn't understand what else I might mean. Please know that when I use it in this book I do not mean "lesser than."

Most people I know use the term *primitive skills* in reference to the making of arts and crafts of "stone age" peoples. With a little digging I determined how this definition came about. Looking through my "primitive skills" books I see that none of them address social-political-educational technologies used by indigenous peoples (except perhaps Tom Brown Jr.). Why? Because most of the authors, like the creators of Rabbitstick, work as "experimental archeologists": scientists who focus on "stone age" handmade tool replication. Not anthropologists, mythologists, or theologists, but archeologists — those who study the physical artifacts of primitive peoples. Unfortunately this definition of primitive skills excludes the social systems that make indigenous societies uniquely different from civilization. Anyone can yield "stone age" handmade tools, including "stone age" civilizationists.

Looking at the diversity of people who attend primitive skills gatherings, from the dirty, earth-loving hippies to the sexist, racist homophobes (who care nothing for the ecology of the planet, let alone their own bioregion), exemplifies how dis-connected from the land these gatherings can feel. When you start to examine indigenous systems, you realize the socio-political prejudice that exists within the minds of civilizationists. For example, if you learn and teach "indigenous mentoring," you can't help but clash with civilization's compulsory schooling model. This makes teachers and supporters of modern schooling (both liberals and conservatives) very upset. If you teach teambuilding and awareness of the land, you rub civilized people (who perceive the world as dead or put here for "Man" to consume) the wrong way. Basically, when you examine social systems it causes a lot of controversy. A great example of this exists on the paleoplanet forum, dedicated to discussing the replication of primitive tools. They created a category called "Primitive Living Experiences," and the head moderator shut it down after people began to argue over the how and why.

No one censored me at a gathering when I talked about civilization's collapse (in fact, a lot of like-minded folks chimed in). But similarly, no one will censor the rednecks who voice their hatred of illegal immigrants. You'll find the slang word *abo* (short for aboriginal) thrown around along with stupid caveman jokes. I can't help but feel sad and angry as I see some of these archeologists and laymen perpetuating the racist stereotype of civilization's caveman mythology: grunting white people with scraggly hair and badly tailored buckskin clothes (common in movies such as *Quest for Fire* or *Encino Man*). White "stone age" cavemen had only bioregional differences from other "stone age" indigenous peoples such as Native Americans. To make jokes about how stupid and shabbily our ancestors must have lived implies that all "stone age" peoples have little intellect. Which obviously shows us why they all didn't build civilizations, right? One of my favorite civilized delusions involves archeologists hypothesizing that "early humans" must have "discovered fire by accident." Just as I imagine modern astronauts must have "accidentally" built a spaceship and flew it to the moon. They can't fathom that "stone age" people had the same level of intelligence that civilized people do.

Since humans make up the systems they live in, when you begin to examine other systems that work better, you come up against cultural prejudices and mythologies that those systems have in place to prevent people from wanting to use another one. Even if you can prove with physical evidence that the other system works better. "Primitive skills," when defined as *replicating physical artifacts*, do not push any real civilized buttons or encourage any kind of social change.

From a rewilding perspective, the *how* and *why* lie at the heart of these skills. If you want to live sustainably you cannot separate tool-making from cultural systems (aka politics) and sense of place (aka religion). Take away the *how* and *why* and these tools become weapons of destruction. For example, anyone can harvest anything anywhere at any time. Know what plants to eat? Great. Eat them. But do you know the most ecologically beneficial time of year to harvest them? You made a bow and some arrows? Cool. But do you know which deer to kill to strengthen the herd? You can't separate ecology from handmade tools. Do you know the best places to gather in your area during the right seasons? Do you have a tribe of people to efficiently gather those plants? Does that group have songs and customs that make the tedious work of gathering more fun? Does your group have a system to distribute food equally among the people? To assume that donning buckskins and making a bow and arrow makes you a hunter-gatherer shows a great underestimation of the vast wealth of culture and expert knowledge of indigenous peoples. It also makes you an asshole.

I have found that many people do not understand how hunter-gatherers blend into the ecology of their place. Hunting and gathering does not mean killing whatever, whenever. A lion does not kill just anything whenever it wants. It does not hunt down the strongest buck; it takes the sick and the weak. Its instincts tell it to thin the herd. Nomadic hunter-gatherers did not simply wander the landscape aimlessly in search of food, taking what they knew they could eat, whenever and however they pleased. Humans have externalized their instincts of what to take, when appropriate and why, into cultural mythology and storytelling (aka spirituality and religion). They moved through the same seasonal circuits, the same places, year after year, tending them the same way any other wild animal would. They kept these routines alive through stories, adapting and changing them with the landscape.

As a bioregional extremist, I feel like primitive skills

gatherings work as nonbioregion-specific handmade-tool gatherings. For those who dream of a culture of rewilding, primitive skills gatherings feel like a great starting place. I don't think of them as "good" or "bad." They merely serve a function: a place to learn handmade primitive arts and crafts from highly skilled practitioners and meet other people who love these crafts. Sure, you may find a re-wilding friend wedged between a Mormon and a Rainbow Child, but you won't find the group intention of learning the skills in the holistic sense and purpose that rewilding encompasses.

For that, we need to start our own bioregion-specific rewilding gatherings, where we don't have to waste time arguing with right wing religious nuts about whether or not civilization will collapse, but can start building communities of people aware of, and no longer in denial of, civilization's inherent unsustainability, who wish to toss the shackles of domestication for the beautiful systems of living that promote biodiversity and environmental integrity.

Resistance vs. Rewilding

When I think of "resistance movements," I envision a small group of people resisting a much larger and all-powerful militarized machine. If I think of civilization as an all-powerful death machine, the idea of resisting it makes me feel small and paralyzed. But when I view resistance through the eyes of rewilding, it looks and feels very different to me.

Civilization works as a way of life that attempts to domesticate, to tame, to make dependent, to enslave the whole world. It fuels its population growth through the domestication of grains. It cannot exist without domestication. It also must work constantly to make its domesticated members so: brainwashing people through television and schooling, genetically engineering plants, growing meat in petri dishes, etc. Civilization does so much work to keep the world domesticated because domestication works as a form of resistance against the natural flow of the world, which always wants to rewild.

When a tree's roots slowly tear up concrete, the tree does not resist the concrete, the concrete resists the tree. The tree just lives its life the way all wild things do. Plants do what they can with their resources to keep the world wild. Dams resist the natural flow of a river. Over many thousands of years, if left alone, the water would whittle the dam down to nothing. The water never resisted the dam. It only did what water does to keep the world wild.

Populations of wild plants and animals that wild humans could eat for food have nearly disappeared through civilization's domestication. Wild humans, as elements integral to the landscape, require an undomesticated land in order to live. If we mean to rewild, it implies that, like the water and trees doing what they can to rewild the planet, rewilding humans need to use their unique, inborn abilities to rewild the world.

For example, civilization has domesticated the Columbia River and all her tributaries, killing nearly all the wild salmon who once lived there. If Cascadians want to live as wild humans, they will need to rewild the Columbia River. Of course, the river itself works as fast as its water can to break away the dam. Unfortunately for the fish and other members of Cascadia, the water alone cannot work fast enough to rewild the river. But rewilding humans, whose ability to make tools comes as naturally as a tree's ability to grow roots, can work much faster to undomesticate that river.

In *The Tales of Adam*, Daniel Quinn uses a metaphor about a wounded lion. If a wounded lion starts killing more than it needs, Adam (a hunter-gatherer) says he will hunt down the lion and kill it because "that is a lion gone mad." Worried the lion would wreak havoc on the entire ecosystem, he would hunt it and kill it so as to prevent that from happening. I doubt that hunting lions felt like a favorable task that any ordinary person would partake in...especially lions gone mad, as they no doubt have less predictability than sane lions. Such a task would definitely not look like the tribesman going about his daily business, but it would fit in with the daily business of maintaining and caretaking the land.

Like the wounded lion who kills at random and takes more than it needs, civilization behaves as a culture that has "gone mad." Like the hunter who has the guts and the skills to hunt down and kill that lion, for rewilding humans with the guts and the skills to remove a dam, it would not look like an ordinary day of pruning a perma-culture garden or checking trap-lines. Yet it would still fit in with the daily business of maintaining and caretaking the land. Hunting down a lion did not require a big military operation (though to smaller-scale indigenous peoples it may have felt like such). But removing a dam may require something on a grander scale.

I think people will decide such actions by whether their band of rewilding humans stands at the front lines of civilization's boundary or the farther reaches out of civ-ilized control, as well as how far civilization's domes-tication reaches into others' landbases. For example, though someone may live in the Canadian Rockies, far from militarized civilization, as long as those dams on the Columbia River stay intact, they prevent salmon from getting to the Rockies. This means that the Rockies still fall under civilization's control. If the natives of old had dammed the river and disallowed other natives upriver from receiving fish, you can bet some shit would have gone down. Similarly, if humans plan to rewild in the Rockies, they'll need to think about how civilization can keep them domesticated from afar. Of course, if we take into consideration the civilization-induced climate crisis, we see that civilization will try to keep us domesticated no matter where we rewild...

Many argue over whether actions like blowing up a dam will bring down civilization or merely strengthen it. To wild humans, an argument like this makes no sense. Like arguing over whether the tree whose roots tear up the sidewalk will bring down civilization or strengthen it. Yes, the tree may get cut down and the street repaved. But civilization will never have the power to cut them all down, to repave all of those streets. A dandelion growing in a suburban lawn, a tree ripping apart the street, an earthquake tearing down buildings, and rewilding humans dismantling logging equipment seems as natural a process as taking out the trash feels to the civilized. I see resistance to domestication as the wildness deep down in our souls bursting forth; a rewilding human blowing up a dam as the natural world going about its daily routines...with a little tenacity.

Many proponents who argue against such actions say that "civilization will just rebuild." The idea that civilization will go on resisting the roots of a tree, cut it down, and pave another road, does not stop the tree from growing roots. Similarly, whether or not civilization will continue to resist the flow of water and build another dam does not stop the actions of rewilding humans. The forces of nature at work, whether we mean trees growing roots, water rushing to the ocean, or wild humans caretaking the land, will continue to undomesticate the world regardless of civilization's growing or diminishing resistance to them.

The mythologists of civilization use the actions of rewilding humans to further their own destruction and may hunt down and kill rewilding humans, but they will never kill them all. Deep down we all have the genetic code to live wild lives, despite the external memetic system of domestication that most of us currently subscribe to. As civilization collapses, more people will realize the need to rewild and will have more and more success rewilding body, mind, river, country, forest, farm, and city, whether they call it rewilding or not.

Of course, you don't necessarily need to blow anything

up. As long as you remove civilization and rewild the river. I think it comes down to scale, bioregion, and in particular, rewilding groups having discussions about their place. Do Cascadians need to rewild the Columbia to have a softer crash in Cascadia? If so, how does one rewild the river? How urgently does this need to happen? How can we do this as quickly and thoughtfully as possible?

When I turn the term *resistance* on its head and see it as civilization resisting the powers of nature, I feel more empowered to resist civilization's domestication. The more I rewild, the less I see *resistance* as resistance but just living and caretaking the land, the way a tree's roots just keep growing and tearing up streets. Sure, civilization may cut some of us down, but it does not have the power to resist the flow of the wild world indefinitely. It will fail, and as rewilding humans, we can help speed that failure up. When we rewild and join with the other wild forces of the world, we become unstoppable.

Pacifism vs. Rewilding

Philosophically I loathe pacifism. Instinctively I would never even consider it. Yet reflexively I enact pacifism when attacked, threatened, or intimidated. I have pacifist values, not because I want or choose to, but because of my training from early childhood in civilization and specifically in school. We learn to never fight back or we will receive worse than the violence we gave. If we wish to fully rewild, we must rewild our relationship to violence.

In order for things to live they have to eat, which means they have to kill. Whether you kill a plant or an animal, you use violence to do it. I don't judge violence as "good" or "bad" because I see it as a function of nature. Like it or not, we cannot escape it. No animals live pacifist lives except domesticated ones (and even then, when given the opportunity...). I see violence in the wild and it looks beautiful to me. We must kill to eat. Life implies violence through death. It can look ugly if you fear death or look beautiful if you embrace it.

The question of violence or no violence bores the shit out of me, really. I accept violence as a beautiful part of our nature, not some grotesque animalistic quality that we left behind when we started building civilization (we just traded in violence for abuse). Do you use violence in a sustainable way, like that of a wild animal, or do you use it in an unsustainable way to further civilization's domestication? "What?" you say. "You can use violence in a sustainable way?" Yes, you can. Chew on that for a bit.

I also don't have a problem with violent communication. When two bucks bash their racks together, they may act violently towards each other, but the violence does not look abusive. It looks real and raw and beautiful. Yes, communication can look violent and not feel abusive. Really, I think we need to learn nonabusive, violent communication. Our culture conflates abuse with violence because those in power control us by using violence or the threat of violence. To live as a domesticated human means to live by the wishes of rulers or *face the consequences.* Killing a life differs from torturing a life into submission. We have a name for that kind of violence: abuse.

If people use violence to take down civilization, it does not work the same way as civilization using violence to force you to live in civilization. Civilization will kill this planet if it doesn't come down. Civilization attacks the whole world every day. If you counterattack civilization to bring it down, it works as a defense mechanism to end domination. *Violence does not beget abuse.* See the difference?

You cannot live as a pacifist and rewild. Those who wish to rewild without bringing down civilization do not understand what rewilding implies. Those who don't see how rewilding implies bringing down civilization don't understand rewilding either. By rewilding, you put yourself against the forces of civilization that work to domesticate the planet. If you don't want to use violence to rewild (I sure don't! I swear it!), you might consider how you will meet that violence when it comes. Without question, visible violence will come knocking at your door at some point or another. Civilization, the collective group of people who perpetuate this way of life, will not quietly put down their weapons and allow you to put a halt to their death wish of domestication. We need to rewild our relationship to violence, retraining ourselves to fight back so that when the time comes we won't reflexively kneel to our masters and allow them to chop off our heads.

Now go put on that one track from the score to *The Last of the Mohicans* (you know the one), paint your face green and black, and brainstorm a battle cry: "Freedom!?!" Sorry...mixing too many movies here.

"Primitive" Living vs. Rewilding

So you want to live like a pure, modern, technology-free hunter-gatherer, huh? In order to do that we need to remove the barriers civilization has in place to stop us from fully rewilding. If we wish to remove these barriers, we must first identify them. The following list shows many of the barriers I have come in contact with. The list feels incomplete, but it covers much of the basics. It also reflects the "pure" end of the rewilding spectrum: those who live so far from civilization (culturally) that they no longer use any industrial-made tools or interact with the civilized economy at all. The most basic survival course covers your immediate needs: shelter, water, fire, and food. We'll start with how survivalists acquire these skills versus how the hunter-gatherers of the Northwest Coast acquired them.

Every barrier falls under one of two categories: violence (aka "the law") or scarcity. Under the barrier of violence, civilization will exert physical force on you for breaking their laws. Think of how the mafia makes businesses pay them for "protection," which really means they won't steal from the business. In the same way, we pay the government for the same kind of "protection." We call this payment "taxes." If we don't pay them, or behave the way they tell us to, they will send the cops to shut us down or throw us in prison. Tell me how that differs from the mob. Under the barrier of scarcity, the lives (such as salmon) that we eat in order to live sustainably now have dwindling populations thanks to civilization's various forms of violence to the planet (in the case of salmon, actual concrete barriers called dams).

Shelter

Materials

If rewilding simply meant "survival," as so many people think, I could build a small debris shelter. But where will my family sleep? Where will my culture sleep? A debris shelter works great for a lone scout who needs to stay on the move. But for a larger culture of people, who plan to hang out longer than a few days, we need something more substantial and homey. Most Northwest Coast Indians slept in thatched huts during the summer months, but in the winter they lived comfortably in long-houses made of western red cedar planks that they could remove from old-growth trees without killing them. This process requires a team of people, a whole set of primitive tools, including wedges, hammers, and ladders, and lots of local old-growth cedars. In order to live in shelters like the natives did here, we would need all of those things. Unfortunately, I don't think I've ever seen an old-growth cedar large enough to get even one good plank out of, let alone enough to construct an entire longhouse. The temperate rainforest of the Northwest rots most natural materials rather quickly. Cedar lasts because of the anti-fungal tannins in the wood.

The precivilized, undomesticated, sustainable economy no longer exists and will take a long time (at least a few hundred years for cedar trees to become old enough for sustainable harvesting) to return, if ever. So much material already exists now; it seems like most houses have one person living in them. Think of all the wasted space! We don't have a rewilding economy, but we do have what we already have here in civilization. We don't need to create more industrial products; we can use the ones already created to hold us over as the economy changes back to a wild one.

Location

Civilization will not let you set up a shelter just anywhere. You need to first have land or property, which means you have to pay money for it. Then you must get a building permit in order to construct your shelter. If you don't go through these avenues, civilization feels it has the right to (and probably will) kick you out of wherever and tear down your shelter. Most camping laws prohibit people from setting up a camp for any period of time more than a few weeks, and in some cities, like Portland, you can't camp at all. This means you have to stay on the move, which means you need some form of transportation for your shelter, unless you plan to build a new one at each site, which again would most likely break the law of energy conservation.

Storage and Security

Something a survival shelter has little to nothing of. These longhouses also stored much food, clothing, and other supplies and (most importantly in the Northwest) kept them dry and rot-free. Oftentimes the survivalist concept doesn't include security of possessions (except for maybe securing minimal food from bears or other animals). Security and storage of your "stuff" becomes an increasing concern when living in more densely populated areas, and even more so the smaller the number of people in your group. For example, if someone always sits watch over the stuff, you've got pretty good security. But if you have to leave items unwatched in a densely populated area, you may not see those items again. Usually we don't think about this because all of our items have twenty-four-hour security locked away in our homes. But if you don't have a home, or you don't have a lock, security becomes a major issue. Especially as the more set up you get in terms of tools, dried foods, and other supplies for an authentic hunter-gatherer culture (and not some week-long excursion in survival), then you end up acquiring a lot more stuff to account for. You need the right tool for the right job, and sustainable hunting/gathering/horticulture, depending on bioregion, can require lots of different tools. Don't believe me? Just read Hilary Stewart's books *Cedar*, *Indian Fishing*, and *Stone, Bone, Antler and Shell*. You don't want to spend hours and hours grinding down a stone wedge only to have it disappear!

Water

Purity

Before civilization brought its pestilence of domestication to the Americas, indigenous peoples could drink water right from streams and rivers. These days, bacteria live in almost all water sources. Once you take a drink, it will cause you some serious indigestion, and if untreated, the water can kill you. Unless you drink from a spring, you need to boil your water. Boiling, however, does not remove Prozac, dioxin, estrogen, and the numerous other industrial-made toxic compounds now found in most water sources. Even the safest water, tap water, often contains chlorine, fluoride, and/or arsenic. If you live in an urban environment it makes much more sense to drink tap water due to fire laws and fuel scarcity, as well as all the other chemicals in the ground in urban places you can't boil out. This generally means you have to pay for water or steal it. Some can find free water in local fountains, but it limits your ability to move freely as you have to stay in close proximity to your water source unless you find a way to contain it. I have, however, also heard of police harassing homeless people for filling containers with water from public drinking fountains. So the threat of violence increases by stealing water or drinking from public fountains.

Transportation

If you must boil water every time you need to drink it, that means you'll not only need fuel for a fire, and a fireproof container to boil the water in, but also a fire-starting device. This means you'll need a system where you have multiple fire-making sets and fireproof containers at various water sources. This increases your security problems as someone such as a cop, other vagrant, or garbage clean-up crew might steal, break, or throw away your tools while you're away. If you decide to carry your water with you, you'll need a container like a water bladder. This goes for all of your tools. Will you carry them with you to every location? Or will you spend the time making and hiding new ones for each location?

Fire

Fuel

In the woods this issue doesn't come up as much, but it can. In the city organic debris such as branches and

twigs that fall to the ground usually get shipped out and
composted somewhere far off. I have tried to gather all my
own firewood for cooking, water purification, and heat,
and it proved very difficult. Unless you want to spend all
your time searching for firewood, which you can't, you
won't have enough to sustain yourself in an urban environment. This means you have to use industrial machines,
which means you have to use gas or electricity.

Location

In the woods, again, this issue doesn't really matter unless
a fire ban exists. But in the city you can't just start a fire
anywhere. If the law allows you to do it in a park, you
usually need a fire pan that sits at least six inches above
the ground. This means another piece of industrialization
you have to carry around. I know some people who have
dug a hole in their backyard, but I don't know the legality
of that. Even then, if you use a backyard, that means
someone pays rent or a mortgage or property taxes, which
means you still support the industrial economy.

Stealth

Fire makes you high-profile. During the day the sight and
smell of smoke, and during the night the light from the
fire, can arise suspicions from people who will contact
"the authorities." Anything that attracts more attention to
your way of life could mean more interactions with the
authorities, and we don't want that!

Flora food

Pollution

Many plant foods and medicines contain toxic amounts of metals, especially those that reside near the roadside or railroad tracks. Many people use pesticides or chemical fertilizers in their yards, so eating plants from that source will make you sick.

Subsistence

Many wild edibles do not suffice for plant subsistence; you can't thrive eating only dandelion greens. The soil in many areas has so many toxins and so few nutrients that the plants themselves may not have much. The native cultures in the Portland area survived mainly off of the wapato tuber through the wintertime. The wapato used to thrive along the Willamette River. When the valley's Indian populations declined almost 90% in the 1830s due to disease, with no one to tend to them and with the introduction of agriculture and invasive species, the wapato nearly died out. It still lives in a few places along the river. This story illustrates that returning to a diet of native plant foods, or even trying to subsist from wild plant food sources on a cultural scale, would prove difficult at this time. Anyone interested in this lifestyle needs to focus on habitat restoration.

Fauna food

Pollution

Toxins, stored in fat, move up the food chain. Animals store more toxins than plants.

Subsistence

As with our plant brothers and sisters, the main animal eaten here in the Northwest by native peoples, the salmon, lies on the verge of extinction.

Permits

In order to hunt and trap most animals, you need to purchase permits. You also cannot use primitive methods, which means you must buy industrial-made traps, guns, or arrowheads.

We haven't even covered more advanced, long-term necessities such as health and hygiene. Where do you shit? What about medicine? What about bathing? The myth that hunter-gatherers didn't have a complex economic system stands as the main barrier here. When you actually sit down and visualize a complex primitive culture, as opposed to a survival scenario, you begin to recognize the near impossibility and undesirability of attempting to live this way under the thumb of civilization, with the constant threat of violence and painful exhaustion from expending too much energy to gather what you need in a 100% primitive, truly "off-the-grid" kind of way. At this point it would not reflect the authentic hunter-gatherer lifestyle we've seen, but rather the suffering lifestyle of the survivalist. We need to look for ways of leveraging the current civilized economic system against itself, towards a hunter-gatherer one. We need to invent an entire rewilding economic system. It really does take a village to rewild! This shows how concepts like permaculture and the Transition Town movement can really help us start building rewilding cultures.

Permaculture vs. Rewilding

I know a lot of "permaculturalists." I've seen many "permaculture" gardens. I have my permaculture design certificate. The problem with my perception of permaculture stems, I think, from the urbanization of permaculture and the terminology used in the books. When I open the books and read phrases like "sustainable agriculture," I shut the books. Because in my experience it doesn't matter how much you teach people about subsistence practices if you don't articulate the problems of civilization simultaneously. Author Toby Hemenway has written the only permaculture texts I've seen that include a critique of civilization. (More probably exist, but not popularly.)

Most commonly when I see people practicing permaculture in the city I see people clinging to the false hope that their garden will save civilization. It's not that I lack knowledge of permaculture or need to read more. The language in the reading says volumes.

In permaculture, *sectors* refers to external influences on your permaculture land. This includes weather, topography, and cultural systems such as laws. Because most permaculturalists do not understand or articulate the sectors of civilization, hierarchy, class, wealth, race, and empire, they don't understand what prevents people from using permaculture to "save humanity."

If, by itself, permaculture examined the unspoken assumptions and unarticulated toxic mythology of civilization, pro-civilization permaculturalists would not exist. Rewilding differs from permaculture in that it refers to a context of ecological principles that challenge the mythology of civilization. Without that context of ecological principles, the skills take on the dominant culture's mythological context and therefore have little to do with rewilding. And if the skills have little to do with undoing domestication, they have everything to do with continuing domestication.

Permaculture works great for a rewilder. Someone can use permaculture as a tool for rewilding, but permaculture itself doesn't reach outside the framework of civilization. If it did, all permaculturalists would understand how civilization controls us. Because most permacultural texts and culture have more to do with design and lack the articulation of how and why civilization kills the planet, civilized people easily miss the implications.

I have had a hard time understanding what permaculture aims to do because of the terminology used in the books and the actions of the people within the subculture. The words used to describe permaculture often obfuscate its real intentions, and further confuse the civilized and rewilders alike. Aside from the general pro-civilization/pro-agriculture language, the subculture of urban permaculturalists has also given rise to my own misinterpretation. At the permaculture events I have attended in the metropolis where I live, I have seen little discussion of walking away from or tearing down civilization and much discussion about how permaculture can save civilization (for example, the widely known and cherished City Repair Project, which bills itself as "Permaculture for Urban Spaces").

If people say that you can have permaculture in urban spaces, either permaculture doesn't mean what I think it does, or those people don't understand permaculture. If we could see permaculture as a design science for creating horticultural villages, we would know you cannot permaculture cities. Cities have a fundamentally unsustainable quality: nothing will make cities sustainable. If permaculture means to render the land sustainable, how would anyone get the idea that you can permaculture a city? Probably because of quotes from local Portland papers like this one:

> A reformed Nordstrom addict, Van Dyke, 56, now teaches "permaculture"—which, practically speaking, means forgoing the lawn in favor of a big, messy garden.
>
>   — *Willamette Week*, August 13, 2008

A couple of fruit trees in your yard and a small garden of self-seeding annuals will not feed you and your hungry neighbors (though it will soften the crash of civilization slightly). The population density of a city far exceeds its carrying capacity, even if every yard has a messy garden instead of a lawn. While you can use the *design principles* of permaculture to plan your urban garden, this misses the point and obscures the intentions of permaculture (if the intention means to create a horticultural-hunter-gatherer culture). If you can't fully feed yourself with your urban permaculture garden, you still require the importation of resources from the countryside. If every farm became a permaculture farm, we could not sustain the populations in the city because permaculture doesn't create excess (grain) food production that makes cities possible. This means that cities would collapse. *If everyone took permaculture to its intention, civilization would collapse.*

Civilized people have lived for thousands of years, forced by a military to farm monocropped grains. Those in power will not allow real permaculture (meaning the full extent of permaculture's intentions to create horticultural-hunter-gatherer cultures) even though permaculture does a great job of reframing indigenous horticulture and making it appealing to the masses who still think hunter-gatherers spent their lives hungry and in constant search for food. As long as civilization holds a monopoly on violence, it owns you and your permaculture farm, and requires the calories of grain production to keep its force. When the time comes, that excess you had for trade will go to the military so that they can kick your ass and hold you captive. I don't see these issues addressed by permaculturalists or in permaculture literature.

Some people say, "Don't listen to what the books say. Look at what people do." But when I look at what the people who make permaculture popular among urban people do, I see people clinging to civilization and calling it permaculture. While I think permaculture design attempts to abandon civilization as a subsistence strategy, without articulating in its own literature the systems that keep us stuck here, permaculture brings civilization along for the ride, and civilization kills the idea before it has the chance to break free.

Rewilding refers to the process of undomesticating ourselves so that ideas like permaculture can and will live up to their potential: creating biologically diverse landbase, seasonally maintained by horticultural-hunter-gatherers, free of civilization. Rewilding offers a kind of sector analysis to describe the culture that understands the power of unarticulated abuse and domination from civilization. It seeks to understand these invisible and visible shackles outright. Once we articulate the problems and control mechanisms of civilization, permaculture becomes one of our strongest allies. But as long as permaculture remains a design science without articulating civilization, it will continue to lose meaning through the urban people who use it to perpetuate false hopes.

Veganism vs. Rewilding

Most recently I've seen this notion that we can change the world by changing our diet, specifically to a vegan diet. I have found that many vegans throw their dietary ethics at others the way Christians throw their spiritual ideology. If you want to eat only veggies, fine. But why the attitude? Why the hate? If you think you have an ethically pure diet, think again. In fact, your diet may worsen the environment.

Some vegans claim they like how they feel on the diet. Others simply say they don't like the taste of meat. But most vegans I know eat that way because of ethics more than for health benefits or personal taste. For this reason, veganism generally falls into an ideological "right" vs. "wrong" category for living, causing most members of the vegan military to demand that everyone else stop their "evil" ways and adopt vegan values. But where do these values come from? And do these espoused values actually make a change in the ways they intend?

Animist peoples experience plants as having feelings too. Just because you don't hear their screams, and can't look into their eyes when you cut them, doesn't mean plants don't feel pain and bleed in a way outside of our perception. The idea that plants somehow have lesser value than animals comes from a nonanimistic view of the world: a civilized, hierarchical view. They don't look like us, they don't grow like us, and therefore they get cast to the bottom of the spiritual hierarchy (at the top of which sits the brains of white men).

I feel terrible for domesticated animals (pets included here). I feel equally terrible for domesticated plants. I feel terrible for anything domesticated (rocks, clouds, air, ideas, etc.). Domesticated crops require domesticated bees for pollination. This implies that vegans consider bugs lower on their spiritual hierarchy. Farmers routinely kill animals like rabbits, crows, and coyotes who enter their fields. Crops kill wild animals too, and force bees into domestication.

In response to this, many vegans might say, "Well, I have chosen veganism to protest factory farming, which causes a lot more degradation to the environment than growing crops. You don't need meat to survive."

It appears to me that population growth lies at the "root" of environmental degradation. "Development" wouldn't happen if we had fewer people. The destructive scale of factory farming would not exist if our population did not grow exponentially. So we need to look at what makes our population grow.

As a teenager I worked at an organic food store and ate a vegan diet. I remember seeing a vegan product that boasted, "Eating vegan helps save food resources for seven people a day." How they calculated that I'll never know, or believe. While most people would see that label and believe their purchase helped the "fight against hunger," I look at it and see that they've only just made seven more hungry mouths to feed.

Domestication of both plants and animals requires defor-estation. But the population explosions that form civi-lizations come from the domestication of grains, not live-stock. The Incas had quinoa, the Aztecs had amaranth, the Mayans had corn, the Chinese had rice, and Whitey had wheat (and now soy). Grain-based diets cause exponential population growth. Population growth increases the scale of everything, turning small ranches into factory farms, turning the local market into a McDonalds. Grain-based diets make factory farms possible. They make "development" possible. They make civilization possible. If everyone switched to a vegan diet, our population would grow that much faster, the destruction that much worse. Vegans constantly say, "You don't need meat to survive." I never hear them follow up with, "Only through agricultural globalization does this become possible."

If you live in North America (or anywhere outside of the jungle), you need meat to survive outside of the grain-based diet of civilization. And so what? Humans have eaten meat for a long time and found sustainable ways to kill that honored the animals, the same as any other predator. Along with sustainable ways to kill plants that honored their lives. Along with sustainable ways to honor stones, weather, and all the other elements of the community. I think the comment "You don't need meat to survive" includes both points I have made: civilization fuels itself on wheat, not meat, and (most) vegans perceive animals as higher on a spiritual hierarchy of suffering.

Want a diet based on anti-civilization ethics? Want to stop supporting the destructive culture? Want to stop population growth? Stop buying processed food at the supermarket. Hunt, gather, garden, buy or trade locally. Give back to the land and quit eating the very thing that makes all of this possible: *grains.*

Personally I eat mostly "paleo," and I don't care if you or anyone else does. My diet works for me, but I don't think that I have found the "one right diet" for all to eat. Though I perceive them, I haven't chosen my diet for ethical reasons. I've chosen it because I feel good eating this way. I understand that just because I feel good eating this way, not everyone else will, as each of us has a particular body with particular needs. If veganism makes you feel good, by all means. But please stop promoting veganism based on false ethics of ceasing the destruction inherent in grain-based diets. I bought into it in my teens (I ate a vegan diet for two years) and won't fall for the mythology again.

As you may imagine, I received many e-mails from pissed-off vegans after posting "Civilization Found in Vegan Ethics." One person just couldn't understand the funda-mental connection between grain diets and population growth. Others, like the ones I responded to here, live in denial that plants have feelings too. I would like to say that some very nice nonfundamentalist vegans and I had a good dialogue, too—thank you, guys!

> Dear Scout,
>
> How can plants feel pain? They have no ner-vous system. The reason that you can't hear their screams is because they have no mouths, vocal cords, etc. For me, I place bugs lower on my hierarchy because they have many less neural con-nections than, say, a chicken or pig. So, I would think that there is less "substance" to them. I mean, come on man, what kind of thinking is it to think that an oak tree can feel pain? I'm all for stopping industrial civilization, as I believe you are, but to advocate a philosophy such as animism is as foolish as believing that some guy named Jesus who lived 2,000 years ago is going to take you to some fairy land called heaven. You also said, "crops kill wild animals too." If you cared about wild animals why would anyone eat raised animals? The amount of grain, mostly corn, to

feed them causes more land to be plowed (thereby causing more deaths of wild animals) than if you just ate lower on the food chain. Just to make it clear, I do think that the Paleolithic diet is a good thing, relative to most diets. I know and realize that veganism is part of the industrial food system. That is why I try to dumpster dive as much of my food as possible thereby giving less $ to the industrial food suppliers.

And this one:

Dear Scout,

I'm glad you have empathy for plants. But here's the difference between plants and animals: plants are cut down, and we eat them. Now here's the thing: whether it's because god made them that way, or evolution has created it, or whatever you believe: when you cut a plant down, it does not struggle. It falls, and you eat it. That's the difference. When you kill an animal, it fights for its life. It defends its existence. That's the difference.

You know, the BBC reported a few years back that fish can actually (oh my god, get ready) *feel pain*. Listen to this:

The first conclusive evidence of pain perception in fish is said to have been found by UK scientists. This complements earlier findings that both birds and mammals can feel pain, and challenges assertions that fish are impervious to it. The scientists found sites in the heads of rainbow trout that responded to damaging stimuli. They also found the fish showed marked reactions when exposed to harmful substances. The argument over whether fish feel pain has long been a subject of dispute between anglers and animal rights activists.

This, of course, makes no fucking sense. Anyone who has ever gone fishing can see the fear in the fish's eyes and notice that it wriggles uncomfortably, in obvious physical pain as it dangles from a hook. Did we really need to have scientists cut up fish and test them with machines to know they feel pain? Does anyone else see the insanity? We can't trust our bodies, only machines made by our brains. Or more specifically machines made by the brains of white men.

Some of us don't need scientific instruments to understand and feel empathy towards fish and, further, plants. If you can tune in with your sense of empathy, you can "hear" the screams of plants and feel their kind of pain. Furthermore you can do this with rocks, wind, clouds, mountains, the moon, etc.

It all comes down to observation and empathy (the sixth sense we must dull to live in civilization). Animism does not refer to something you "believe" in that you cannot experience or see directly. It refers to observations made using all of your senses (including the sense of empathy) while living in an animate world, about an animate world. It works as a way of perceiving the world based on direct experiences with it. I cannot observe Jesus, his teachings, or a heaven, but I can observe the world around me and its happenings. My perception of animate plants does not come from faith but from direct sensory experience. I'll give you one example:

I sat in my backyard for one hour a day for several months, in the same spot under the dogwood tree with the robin's nest. Every day I would sit and practice a sensory meditation, clear my thoughts and relax and watch the natural world of an urban yard unfold before me. Much like watching television, I merely observed and did not interact, though I had a deep sense of wanting to belong. After several months of this I began to wonder if I would ever feel like I belonged. Then one day I sat down and began to enter into the mental space of the sensory meditation. Immediately I felt different. I could sense something completely new. I can't tell you which sense experienced this feeling, but it felt like I had finally become part of the family. I could feel the plants. I could feel the water pulsing up their stalks, and I could feel the energy feeding them from the sun. It felt like they had put their arms around me. I hate using the term *oneness* to describe anything, but it really did feel as though they had let me in on a secret. It felt more like *togetherness*.

The next moment I began to feel afraid. I could feel they felt scared too. Then the neighbor came outside. Somehow I just knew what would happen next. I wanted to run. But I heard something say, "We can't run!" At that point I knew they wanted me to stay. So I stayed there with them as my neighbor weed-whacked his yard, and I cried. Imagine your legs buried in cement and someone begins to cut them off. You can't run, you can't do anything but watch. Imagine your family members stand next to you, and you can do nothing for them. At least animals can run and fight. Actually some plants can too. Thorns, anyone? Poison? But even then, so what if one can run and one can't. I don't discriminate against one more than the other because one has legs and one has roots.

That experience only speaks to me, since I experienced it alone. I trust this experience because nature has no agenda. Of course, my own cultural views can get in the way, but even then I think some sensory experiences can break through cultural worldviews. I know many people who have shared similar experiences with plants (and rocks and trees and wind and everything else). Why then do scientists spend so much time cutting up and torturing fish, and cutting up and torturing plants, looking for hard-core factual, measurable data proving that these things experience pain, when our own bodies, if listened to, can actually communicate with these other-than-humans?

I don't *believe* in animism, I *experience* it, and share my experiences in hopes of inspiring others to seek out similar experiences. We must make animism sound childish in order to see the world as dead.

As for the other comments:

> You also said, "crops kill wild animals too." If you cared about wild animals why would anyone eat raised animals? The amount of grain, mostly corn, to feed them causes more land to be plowed (thereby causing more deaths of wild animals) than if you just ate lower on the food chain.

Again, if the corn, soy, and other grains that currently feed cattle turned into fields for human consumption, that would provide *more* food in the food supply for humans, which means *more* humans. Which means they would bulldoze even more wild lands for grains and houses, cars, oil, and so forth.

I don't claim an ethically pure diet here. I buy most of my food from the store. When I can afford it, I buy local, grass-fed, free-range, hormone-free, etc. Portland has many of those stores, so I don't find that difficult. In order to escape civilization and rewild, we need to figure out how to "unlock the food" from civilization. I want to hunt and gather and garden all my own food. I can't, because I don't know how, and it feels extra hard because no one else does either (at least in this country). Not to mention that civilization has destroyed much of the wild food! No one lives a 100% primitive, wild lifestyle anymore.

> Just to make it clear, I do think that the Paleolithic diet is a good thing, relative to most diets. I know and realize that veganism is part of the industrial food system. That is why I try to dumpster dive as much of my food as possible thereby giving less $ to the industrial food suppliers.

As far as dumpster diving goes, I don't really do much of that either. I dumpster fruit and that's about it. Most of the food I find contains wheat and sugar, which poison my body. I don't eat grains, not because I want to protest the civilized economy but because they totally fuck up my body and make me feel like shit. I don't think of the paleo diet as good, I think of it as the most nourishing food I can put in my body. Other people may experience a different feeling.

A while back a friend of mine came across an article about Natalie Portman, the greenie of the moment. According to the article, Portman enjoys traveling the world and spreading goodness on the off-season, wishes she could ride a bike everywhere, and eats a vegetarian diet. This doesn't sound that strange or new to me. The insanity begins in that every article in every kind of publication lately seems to focus around "green" issues and "green" celebrities. You can't look anywhere without seeing the green bullshit.

One morning I sat down for breakfast and started reading one of the local papers, *Willamette Week*. The feature article that week focused on the ten-year anniversary of the Kyoto Protocol and how, geez, the U.S. sure acts crazy not signing it, you know?! (Snoooore.) Anyway, the article quotes a local vegan storeowner who said:

> I think that people are aware [that veganism is touted as a solution to global warming]. That's

not my motivating factor for being a vegan, but
a lot of big groups are using that as an emphasis
point right now, when people are giving a shit
about their carbon footprint and all that. "Look,
it's not just a bunch of animal-rights people! It's
the U.N.!" I think for the most part, it's not the
people I know's main reason for doing it. It's just
kind of an added bonus.

I got angry, shut the paper, sat there seething in animos-
ity, sipping my Earl Grey tea and thinking, "We are totally
and completely fucked." Then a young woman sat down
at the table next to me. A waitress came up and took her
order. The waitress asked her, "Are you a vegan? Because
our pesto has dairy in it." "Um. Yeah, *I'm vegan*," replied
the girl, proudly and smugly, as though the waitress had
just asked if she starred in the summer blockbuster or
played in some famous band. "Yeah. I have a band. *I'm
cool.*" "Yeah. *I'm vegan.* I'm doing my part to stop global
warming."

The rage I feel at a "solution" that looks worse than the
current system suffocates me. I feel like bursting into
tears, and I do, but the rage often feels too strong. As I said
in "Agriculture vs. Rewilding," grain-based diets stimu-
late a population growth feedback loop. That should look
like enough proof that a vegan diet supports population
explosion, deforestation, desertification, and overall ecological collapse. The second largest reason the Amazon
rainforest experiences clear-cuts involves the growing of
soybeans, a vegan staple. Trees, specifically old-growth
forests, act as the largest carbon-sink in the world. The
Amazon rainforest itself does more to prevent climate
change than anything people can do.

Now some vegans argue that those soybeans actually feed
cattle and not humans. What do you think McDonalds

would do if everyone turned vegan? Do you think they'd call it quits? Fuck no. Instead of feeding soy to bovine cattle for Big Macs, they'd make a McNasty Soy Burger for human cattle. Veganism as a solution to global warming looks as insane to me as corn ethanol does for a solution to peak oil. These do not work as solutions. They work like trying to put out a fire with gasoline. Agriculture has caused all of our problems. So what do we come up with as a solution? More agriculture! Fucking genius. Veganism just cuts out the middleman of meat. Why feed grain directly to cows when you could feed it directly to an ever-growing population of humans? Yes, factory farms fuck shit up. But agricultural farms fuck shit up more and form the foundations for factory farms.

My friend showed me a different article in the same local paper where they interview a vegan "animal rights activist." I couldn't believe it when I read the following line of questioning:

> **WW:** While hunting may seem cruel in America, because it's not necessary for most people's survival, what happens in a culture where people must hunt to survive? Do animals still have the same rights?
>
> **Vegan:** Animals are not on this planet for us to use. There needs to be respect for the fact that they are individual living beings. If people can live without using animals, they should do that.

What about plants? Plants live as individual beings. Do they not deserve respect? How about having respect for the land and not clear-cutting the Amazon to grow your soy or corn monocrop? People can only live without eating animals within the agricultural economy. If people can live without plants or animals or water or air, they should to that too. That sounds like a complete lack of understanding of how whole systems work together. If that sounds dissociative enough, then she drops this bomb:

> **WW:** What about the Inuit in Canada, who help support themselves by hunting?
>
> **Vegan:** I'm not an expert on the Inuit. But if they can mine and sell gas, diamonds, gold, and heavy metals, they can certainly ship in some tofu. If everyone had as much respect for animals and the sacrifice they make for humans as [they do] for native cultures, this world would be a much better place.

"Ship in some tofu?" Okay, okay...I may not have some fancy-shmancy "environmental studies" degree like she does, but I can smell bullshit. Her comment sounds completely racist, because she puts the blame of animal torture on native peoples and their way of life. Let me translate her comment: "If they can have their entire culture destroyed by civilization, then have their landbase destroyed at the hands of the gas, diamonds, gold, and heavy metals corporations, they can certainly eat something that has nothing to do with their lives whatsoever."

Native cultures don't "ship in" food because they live as natives. Native *meaning* "belonging to a particular landbase." We call them natives precisely because they don't ship in food from other lands. Native hunting and gathering cultures did not create factory farming, animal testing, or domesticated animals. These cultures do not "use" animals, they *eat* them. After living sustainably in this way for thousands of years and then having their culture and land destroyed by civilization in a few hundred, now here comes a vegan missionary from civilization telling them they need to stop living from their own landbase and eat tofu made from soy, grown by civilizationists in the deforested region of the Amazon basin, no doubt. All in the name of animal rights? Someone needs to get their priorities straight. Seriously.

Her comment demonstrates no understanding of indigenous philosophy or compassion for their broken and destroyed cultures. That she would even suggest that they import food shows she has no understanding of how their cultures interact with the planet in a sustainable and ethical way. That she would say that indigenous cultures receive more respect than animals sounds just as insane. If you respected indigenous cultures, you would not insult them by telling them they should live the way you do. That sounds like cultural genocide, something they have experienced the world over. Vegetarian and vegan mythology has no real connection to place, nor an understanding of ecological principles of food subsistence and sustainability. Here's another great example:

The day before I last brought author Derrick Jensen to Portland, I got a phone call. It went something like this:

> **Lady:** Hi. I'm calling because I have some questions about the Derrick Jensen talk tomorrow.
>
> **Scout:** Okay, great. How can I help you?
>
> **L:** Well, I'm trying to decide if I should go or not. I'm just curious if Derrick Jensen is vegan or has ever mentioned veganism.
>
> **S:** No. I know he is not a vegan, and I think he has written a little bit about that. I'm sure he'd answer your questions about it if you came tomorrow.
>
> **L:** Well, I don't know if I would have time to say everything now. You see, global warming is a serious problem, and it's caused by factory farming. If everyone turned to a vegan diet, we would—

S: I'm sorry, I disagree with you. But I am not Derrick. If you'd like to ask him about it, I'm sure you can do that tomorrow at the talk.

L: Well, I'm curious what part you disagree with.

(I hesitate, but feel a little vivacious, so I bite.)

S: Well, civilization is fueled through grain-based diets. I am totally against factory farming, but civilization is only possible through the domestication of grains, not animals. If everyone turned vegan it would only fuel more desertification and population growth, which means more consumption of everything.

L: But don't you think that...

(The conversation goes on for about twenty minutes. I tell her that I support animal rights but have nothing against killing animals. She says she doesn't have a problem with people killing animals either, but keeps arguing that somehow veganism will help, even though I've described how it can't. Then she says something about meat being poison, and I say...)

S: Humans have been eating meat for three million years.

L: Well, they've also had slavery for three million years, so just because—

S: That's not true. Slavery only exists within civilizations.

L: Well, just because something has been happening for a long time doesn't mean we shouldn't change it. Women weren't allowed to vote at one time, but that doesn't mean they shouldn't just because they haven't.

S: That has nothing to do with what we're talking about. You just said that meat is poison. We're talking about evolution. Humans have evolved to eat meat.

L: Then I guess you have never read the blah blah blah about how meat does blah blah blah and is poison!

S: Actually, I have read a bunch of that, and it doesn't make any difference, because if it were poison I wouldn't be talking to you right now because we wouldn't have lived for three million years eating it. But that's all beside the point anyway. The point is that humans have eaten meat for three million years and lived in a sustainable, *ethical* way (outside of civilization).

L: Well, humans have also lived as vegans for three million years!

S: No, they haven't.

L: Yes, yes they have! In a *parallel dimension*.

S: ?!?

L: ...

S: This conversation...is over.

(Click.)

I seriously couldn't make this shit up. Even if a vegan dimension exists (giving her the benefit of the doubt here), what the fuck does that have to do with *this* dimension? I don't think she came to the Q and A. I made up my own little Q and A for your entertainment, though. It goes like this:

> **Q:** What do you get when you remove people from their connection to their landbase, make them practice agricultural subsistence, put them in a hierarchical social structure, and wait 10,000 years?
>
> **A:** Racist vegans from Dimension X.

I support animal rights activism insofar as it recognizes the rest of the world too. I support *animist* rights activism. I think all things, humans and other-than-humans, deserve lives free of torture and exploitation: animals, plants, insects, rocks, water, wind, and stars. Of course, activism only becomes necessary when you have a culture that does not recognize that those other-than-humans require respect. "Rights" only become an issue when someone fucks you over and you can do little about it.

Dieting vs. Rewilding

Most of us rewilding people do not yet have the skills or the land to hunt and gather or practice horticulture full-time, or the culture to help us out. And yet undomesticating the food we eat seems at the very heart of rewilding, since the very heart of domestication involves growing our food: the domestication of food spawned the domestication of everything. Converting to a domestic-free diet may prove difficult for many, especially overnight. Lucky for us, ways exist to limit the amount of domestication and the terms of the domestication of the food that we eat without us having to hunt and gather or grow it all ourselves right away. Hunter-gatherer-gardeners eat very different diets than those who practice agriculture. Though diets vary drastically from bioregion to bioregion, basic principles exist to put them into different categories.

Eating a wild diet reduces population growth factors and deforestation

Our modern diets come from practicing agriculture as a means for subsistence. Agriculture refers to a method of growing food that requires simulated catastrophe to inspire first-phase succession plants, specifically grasses like wheat and corn but also other grains, legumes, and some starchy tubers. You cannot grow grasses and grains inside a forest, so people must create a catastrophe (fires, floods, clear-cuts) to clear the forest to plant grass. Without human hands the area would naturally recover over time. This requires constant catastrophe to keep the field from turning back into a forest. When you change the land to grow a monocrop of grains for human consumption, you increase the food capacity of that land for human growth. This in turn causes the population of humans to artificially inflate beyond what the forest would support.

Monocropping creates all kinds of problems. Aside from the extraneous amount of work (constant tilling) it takes to keep the land from turning into a forest, monocropping depletes nutrients in soils and provides the perfect environment for "pests" and disease. Because monocropping has such fragility, people who use this method of cultivation must devise solutions to live through poor yields. *Enter the food surplus.*

In order to combat the ills of agriculture, people invent prolonged food storage, which leads to rampant population growth, which leads to more cutting of forests to grow more grains for food storage, which leads to more population growth, which leads to *civili-fucking-zation.* A positive feedback loop of *grain fetishization* and *baby booming.*

Not all food planted in the ground can provide people with the protein that causes population growth. You cannot feed a large population with leafy greens. By choosing not to eat grains, you make the choice to stop supporting the plants that make population explosion and deforestation happen. Notably, a lot of deforestation these days involves cutting forests down to graze cattle. However, cattle themselves take up land that could otherwise feed more people if they grew grains on the land instead, not to mention the grains they must feed the cattle themselves. Animal domestication does not inspire population growth. Even the vegans say that (vegan.org):

> In a time when population pressures have become an increasing stress on the environment, there are additional arguments for a vegan diet. The United Nations has reported that a vegan diet can feed many more people than an animal-based diet. For instance, projections have estimated that the 1992 food supply could have fed about 6.3 billion people on a purely vegetarian diet, 4.2 billion people on an 85% vegetarian diet, or 3.2 billion people on a 75% vegetarian diet.

Whoever wrote this does not understand the connection between population growth and grain production. Veganism, while addressing many of the terrible problems with animal cruelty and polluting factory farms, does not address the larger force that drives population growth. In fact the diet simply adds more *fuel* to the population growth *diet*. By taking grains out of your diet you support another way of food subsistence and limit population growth. I don't want anyone to think that eating differently will "save the world" or "bring down civilization." Changing your diet alone will not help that. It may simply lessen the destruction you contribute as an individual person in civilization, and perhaps make you feel better and healthier when the collapse does occur and most people suffer grain withdrawal.

Eating a wild diet decreases waste products

By eating wild you reduce packaging and plastics. Produce and meat don't generally have a lot of wrappers, and wild foods have none at all. "Yeah, I've got a landfill in my backyard: my compost pile, bitch."

Eating a wild diet probably reduces carbon emissions (buzzword of the year!)

By buying locally you reduce the distance that the food needs to travel. By buying produce and meat (wrapped in paper) you reduce the plastics and energy used to package and preserve foods. Also, wild plant foods rarely need cooking, so you save some energy there too. "I don't do no good at the math." But I can make an educated guess here, no?

Eating a wild diet increases your health?

Let's put our anti-civ ethics aside and just talk about our selfish desire to feel great. Don't get me wrong. I love pizza, cake, and ice cream as much as the next kid. But I also have a wheat allergy (who doesn't, really?) and a lactose intolerance (again, who doesn't?). I love the taste of pizza and the satisfaction of eating it very much, so much that I don't mind the sloppy diarrhea that keeps me up half the night when I eat it. I love it so much I don't mind the constant sinus infections and immune disorder. I don't mind the sore knee joints and itchy skin and swollen lymph nodes and stinky armpits and stomach cramps..."Hmm. Can you put extra whipped cream on my 16 oz bacon and peanut butter milkshake?"

Eating a wild diet makes you...wild!

Eating a wild diet frees you from the civilized economy and reconnects you to your landbase.

And other dietary babble...

Some people theorize that agriculture came about as humans became addicts to the doping effects of grains. Civilization, a culture of drug addicts? Others theorize that the pathogenic, grain-loving microflora that live in our bodies made us crave the grains, which made us practice agriculture. So maybe the microflora controls us. Aaaaaah!

Raw foodists argue that meat also contains poisons that our bodies do not digest well. I don't necessarily disagree with them, so much that...Who fucking cares? The bottom line here does not look like toxins but ecological implications. Humans evolved to digest meat more smoothly long ago. They also evolved to live in "equilibrium" with their particular bioregions that require meat as a protein source...without destroying their ecosystem. So eating meat, toxin or no, has no ill effect on ecosystems. Some people have also developed less sensitivity to grains. However, grain-based cultures must use agriculture to grow those grains, and agriculture causes desertification of the planet. Soooooo what does that tell us?

We should not confuse foods with their production methods. You can grow a few grains in your horticulture garden and eat them occasionally, but when you cut down the whole forest to grow your monocrop of corn, you will begin to experience serious problems.

Your diet will not stop civilization

While we can all dream that simply changing our diet will solve all of the problems we created, unfortunately it won't.

Money vs. Rewilding

I don't consider money the root of all evil, but I fucking hate it. Not because I don't have it, but because people fear living without it. People don't know how to live without it. People don't know what living looks like without it. People feel afraid of losing it. They would rather have money than a community. They would rather live alone and rich than hungry and surrounded by friends. Why?

The million-dollar question: *What replaces money in rewilding?* Money works as a medium of exchange. Dictionary.com tells us that an exchange means "to give up something for something else; part with for some equivalence; change for another." Money symbolizes this exchange. It works as a stored exchange.

What do you need in order to eat in civilization? Money. What do you need to clothe and shelter yourself in civilization? Money. What do you need to entertain yourself in civilization? Money. What do you need to get this money? If you don't have independent wealth, you need a job. In civilization, money equals support.

What does an exchange look like? Giving someone something for something else. Giving something and getting something in return. A trade. Trade seems like a funny word. It means both an exchange and what you do for your livelihood. What do we do for money but trade our bodies and services? To make my money I chop vegetables for other people to eat. I then use the money to pay other people to chop vegetables for me to eat. And why do I buy food at the grocery store? Because I don't know how to get it for myself. We trade our lives for services we cannot provide for ourselves.

An exchange can't happen without people providing a service or a product (which really just means the service of making the product). What does this service represent, really, but the actual person who performs it? Without that person there, you have no service. The person exchanges their time and skills. They exchange hours of their life that they will never see again, to give something of themselves for something in return. The exchange happens not for the product but for the person who made it. An exchange involves people giving support to one another for support they cannot receive by themselves. Neither the product nor the services have any real value. The real value lies in the person who provides the product or service.

This describes the essence of the tribal system that Daniel Quinn articulates in his books: *give support, get support.* In tribal cultures people relied on each other for the basic necessities of life. Each person contributed their time, and in return found all of their needs met. This may reveal why indigenous cultures found wealth in their people, not in the material items they produced.

Money works as a symbolic representation of people, of tribe. We even put pictures of people on our money. In civilization, people do not give you support: money does. That demonstrates how money, although a symbolic representation of people, holds more value than the people making it. It reveals to us why people of our culture seek money more adamantly than they seek actual friendships, and feel more willing to abandon a friendship if it means getting more money. Psychologically, *money means friendship.*

If money serves as the foundation of your support, you will do whatever you can to keep that money or get more. People fear living without it, so they fight to keep it. I have participated in many tribal ventures that have failed. I believe they failed because we could not see the value of people over money. You can take the human out of civilization, but you can't take the civilization out of the human. None of these tribal ventures attempted to operate without money; all of them existed in fear of not making enough. When people feel afraid of not getting enough money, they try to control the money. At that point the hierarchical tendencies of civilized people infiltrate and destroy the group.

I don't mean to say that you can't have a tribe and participate in the monetary economy. If you look to people for support, or geese or salal berries, you will do whatever you can to maintain those relationships and create more. Gypsies use money, but I don't think they value the money they use more than their band. They do not feel afraid of going hungry together, and from what I have read they have no social pressure to become billionaires.

I believe that part of rewilding involves abandoning the value of money over relationships. What do you replace money with? I think the more appropriate question looks like this: what did people have before money? They had a *tribe.* Money feels like a poor, unfulfilling replacement for real people and real relationships. I want to live without money not because I consider myself a "primitivist" but because I would rather have a tribe. Plus, if we can prove to other people that we can do it, hopefully their fear of living without money will dissipate and we will have even more friends to hunt and gather with.

Video Games vs. Rewilding

While cleaning out his room, my buddy Willem found an old USB universal game controller. Basically it looks and works like a PlayStation controller but plugs into your computer. He said it used to belong to his brother and asked if I wanted it. God help me, I said yes.

As a kid I played video games quite often. I did other things too. I wouldn't describe myself as your classic video game nerd or anything, just a nerd who played video games. People have always known me to binge on things. When I drink, I can't have just one. I'll drink until I pass out, piss on someone's couch, or convince someone to punch me in the face (this describes why I no longer drink much at all!). Video games have felt no different. I used to binge on one game and play it for hours. The list, I think, goes like this: *Super Mario Bros.*, *The Legend of Zelda*, *Super Mario Bros. 3*, *Super Mario World*, *Zelda: A Link to the Past*, *Civilization*, *King's Quest* (one through five), *Space Quest* (one through five), *Final Fantasy 2*, *Secret of Mana*, *Chrono Trigger*, *Duke Nukem 3D*, *Diablo*, *Final Fantasy 7*, and a few others. I didn't play a shitload of games, just a small amount very often. At some point I decided it would work best if I just didn't play video games at all, just as I most recently decided that drinking and smoking don't work for me either.

A few years back when I began to formulate my under-standing of the power of mythology and story, I often con-versed on the Joseph Campbell Foundation forum. One day someone brought up video games as a newer medium for mythology. A man argued heavily against this, saying, "Video games are nothing but pure escapism. Something such as entertainment that allows one to escape from their ordinary or unpleasant reality for a time."

The existence of the word *escapism* indicates another symptom of a culture that does not meet our needs: es-capism, the need to escape, requires that one experiences reality as undesirable or unpleasant. No wonder civilized people came up with the term. According to the mythos of civilization, the world lies dead and we as farmers must suffer in this life to go to heaven in the next. Who wouldn't want to escape the abuse this culture tells us we must experience?

This brings to mind the great, lengthy stories told by indigenous peoples around the world, the stories that often take several weeks to tell. Do these stories rep-resent escapism or something else? Does a difference exist between listening to a nine-day-long indigenous myth and watching a twenty-four-hour marathon of *X-Files* episodes? I would argue that they have a similar function—to spread and maintain a culture's myths (or memes)—but differ in their opposing value systems. In-digenous stories connect people to physical reality, en-riching the physical world around them, while civiliza-tion's stories continue to take people further away from physical reality. *X-Files* taught me nothing about the physical land I live on, nor how to live on it in a sus-tainable way. Rather the show focuses on characters and places "alien" to the planet. And while *X-Files* may have actually had *aliens* as characters, you could say the same thing about religious myths that put stock in a heaven and a god as alien to the earth as the "grays." Contrast this with the songlines of the Australian indigenous peoples, which taught them how to move about real places in their land, honor the gods of those places, and participate in a sustainable way with the other-than-human "characters" they met on their travels.

I initially disagreed with the notion that video games work as pure escapism, but the more I think about civilization's mythology, the more I realize how most of it involves escaping our perceived reality. Whether you call yourself a scientist working to find another planet to live on after we trash this one, a Christian who follows the Ten Commandments and goes to church every Sunday in hopes of someday escaping to heaven, or a *World of Warcraft* addict who spends your life in a manmade virtual world, you spend your life trying to escape the physical reality that indigenous peoples and nonhumans seem to love so much. Entertainment works hard at escapism, in addition to drugs, science, and religion. Video games merely act as the newest spokesman for civilization's escapist mythology.

Some civilized people attempt to destroy the myth that this world hates us and that we must suffer in it. Old animist myths sometimes grow above the invasive blackberry thicket of civilization's religions, reminding us the world has a life, a heart that cares and longs for us to remember it back into existence. Ironically, much of the animist mythology that came to me as a child came in the form of video games. Animism still has a presence in modern Japanese culture, and Japanese culture produces a large amount of games. While the physical act of playing video games may take us out of physical reality, some games actually can and do teach or inspire us to connect with the land and defend it against civilization. Therefore, though video games come from civilization (which aims to escape or dominate what it perceives as a cruel and wild world), not all of the video games we play propagate those lies.

This does not negate that civilization created video games, and that it takes an inherently unsustainable, industrial economy to make them. Still, when I look back on my formative years I find that video games had a much deeper impact on the foundations of the choices I make now than I formerly realized.

Merry Christmas Mario

At the age of five I received a Nintendo Entertainment System on the celebration of the Christ's birth. On that day I witnessed the birth of a newer, cooler spiritual leader who came with many faces: Super Mario, Zelda, Donkey Kong. When I turned eleven I received another gift: the life-changing myth they call *Final Fantasy 2*.

Final Fantasy 2 (American Release)

FF2 begins with you (or your character) getting exiled for questioning your king's motives for invading a neighboring community. You thereby lose your rank as the leader of the army. The king gives the task of delivering a small package to a nearby village of summoners (those with the ability to summon earthly creatures). Upon arrival, the package (rigged with a spell) explodes in flame and destroys the entire village. During the fires you only have the ability to help one survivor, a little girl who has just witnessed her whole family and village destroyed by the demons in the package, delivered by you, by order of the king. At this time you realize the king has gone mad and must die. Rydia, the young "caller," joins your newly formed resistance group for the next big chunk of the game. Just when you think everything has worked out, your boat sinks and everyone on your team drowns, including the little girl. You wake up alone, stranded on a distant island.

They called her Rydia, my first love, and when she died I mourned for her. For some reason I sympathized with her so much. Maybe because I felt responsible for killing all her people. Maybe because I related to feeling alone in the world. Maybe because she had cool green hair. Maybe because she befriended the gods. When I lost her, I cried, heartbroken. People say that this "is just a game." I disagree. How do you perceive games? Why do we tell stories? If mythology works as vehicles for understanding spiritual archetypes, certainly games can have much more power than people give them credit for. Rydia felt alive and real, the innocence of the green flowering earth, who summons the elements and converses with gods, and whose people (friends of gods) died by a murderous holocaust that I unknowingly brought upon them by simply doing what those in power told me to. I can't think of a greater metaphor for my role in civilization.

Although not by intention but by my relation to a diseased and jealous king, I still understood it my moral obligation to look after her in an attempt to undue, at the very least, a fraction of the injustice that I, and my culture of kings, had done to her. I didn't cry because a bunch of pixels stopped appearing on the TV screen. I cried because my own spirit died at the hands of my own culture, because I did what those in power told me to do. The loss of her and what she represents in us all: that part of us that still remembers the secret language of the gods. I cried also because the story does not end there. Always we have more story to uncover, more life to live. The world does not die with her but weepily continues. We still have time to save what little life we have left in the world from the greedy evil empire of civilization. I still remember that on my eleventh birthday I saved the world from those who wished to destroy it.

Sid Meier's *Civilization*

I first played *Civilization* over at the Johnsons' house. The Johnsons' house always had wonderful clutter, with all kinds of interesting toys and gismos and contained many distinct aromas that I have never smelled anywhere else. The father carved wood into salmon, and up from the basement always wafted the sweet smell of cedar filling the kitchen where the computer sat. During summer, no matter the time or day of the week, the computer had six or seven neighborhood kids surrounding it, all engaged in feeding our young, curious intellects. Of all the games we played in that house, I remember *Civilization* the most, because it gave me a fundamental understanding of how civilization works: one wins the game by either becoming the first civilization to colonize Alpha Centauri (the closest solar system) or by destroying every other culture on the planet. Your choice: colonization or genocide (two prongs on the same pitchfork). While the game never said anything that goes against civilization, it brought the unspoken premises of our culture to light early on. This created the perfect primer for perspectives I later discovered in reading Daniel Quinn, Derrick Jensen, Martín Prechtel, and others.

Diablo

At fourteen I went to a local store, picked this game off the shelf, and walked out the front door. The buzzers even went off. I kept walking, expecting middle-aged rent-a-cops to bury me in a pig pile any second. I took the long, scenic way home in case someone followed me. A strange form of thievery paranoia I had never felt before came over me, even though I had shoplifted many times before. It felt as though someone (or some*thing*) had come with me from the store. I cradled the box to my chest and hurried on, winding this way and that through the neighborhood streets. When I got home I closed the blinds and watched out the window for hours, unable to shake the feeling that something watched me. A feeling that didn't stop me from sitting down at my computer and installing the game...

Six months later I sat in front of my computer and opened my eyes. I had sacrificed much for this game: what little social life I had, beautiful sunny afternoons spent inside. I suffered as an addict (or escapist). You know that old saying, "You don't smoke cigarettes, cigarettes smoke you." Well, *Diablo* definitely smoked me. At the time I didn't think about the mythic proportions of devils stalking and possessing me. I felt weak from atrophied muscles, looked pale from lack of sunlight, and felt depressed from not having real, physical friends. Then something happened. Maybe I'd had enough, or maybe an angel came to rescue me from the devil. As I fought in a battle deep within the fifteenth level of hell, my left hand lifted from the keyboard and down to the eject button on the CD-ROM. The CD tray slid out in slow motion, like the stone monolith in *2001: A Space Odyssey*. I lifted the CD from its shrine and bent the dense plastic until it snapped into two pieces, one in each hand. I felt something warm trickle down my arm. I had sliced my hand open, and now fresh blood flowed down my left arm onto the CD shard that had given me the wound. I understood what had happened immediately: "If I can't have you, no one can." The last lunge of a dying beast. The ritual scarification of sacrifice. I squeezed my hand and ceremonially bled on the now inanimate, unusable, transformed blades in my hands. "You have no power over me," I whispered, quoting Jennifer Connelly in *Labyrinth*. I had, for the first time, fought back against one of my masters, albeit a mythological master comprised of ones and zeroes.

Final Fantasy 7

After *Diablo* I swore off video games. But then *Final Fantasy 7* came out, and maybe the memories of Rydia told me to break my rule to play this one. Just this one. Derrick Jensen mentioned a movie coming out in which anarchists poison the world's water supply and the government must stop them. He said it would look more realistic if in the movie *corporations* poisoned the world's water (a common practice) and a group of *anarchists* had to stop them. This would threaten civilization's mythological system, however, so games, movies, and other media with those stories rarely make it past the drawing board.

Somehow *Final Fantasy 7* slipped through the cracks. The quest begins with Cloud (the character you play), hired as a mercenary to help a terrorist group blow up a reactor. This reactor (an obvious metaphor for a nuclear reactor) steals the earth's life force (called Mako) for the purpose of powering industrial civilization. After the corporations kill innocent people (and blame the terrorists), your character becomes morally involved with the terrorist group. The rest of the game includes a number of great anti-civilization bits, like courting and befriending indigenous people and rescuing an endangered species from an animal testing lab. Squaresoft created this game before the term eco-terrorist became popular. Years before the Green Scare. When I finished the game I had logged over 100 hours working to take down this make-believe civilization. At fifteen I saved the world all over again, from another civilization. But after the credits rolled, the world I live in still sat waiting for someone to rise up and save it. After having taken down several civilizations, psychologically, perhaps that prepared me to do it for real.

At nineteen I swore off video games (again!) after playing a game called *Hitman*. My brother had it on his computer, and I only played it once for about three hours. During the first three levels, you kill Asian mobsters. When I say "Asian" I don't really mean Asian, but iconic representations of "Asian" facial features. You have to sneak up behind them and kill them. The computer has artificial intelligence that makes them look over their shoulders for you. I spent three adrenaline-fueled hours as the main character, who looks like a white male with a shaved head, killing computer-generated Asians. The next day as I walked in downtown Portland, the crosswalk turned red before I got there. As I approached the corner a man stood waiting. He happened to look over his shoulder at me in a way very similar to the computer-generated characters in the game. He looked Asian. I felt my hand reflexively reaching for a gun to kill him with.

What. The. Fuck!? Anyone who plays down the brain-programming of video games has no idea. Of course the military knows this; you can download a similar game from goarmy.com.

So when Willem gave me the video game controller, I thought it may lead to my end. But for the last several days I have played *The Secret of Mana*, a game similar in plot to *Final Fantasy 7*, and have felt disinterested. I asked myself why I didn't enjoy playing games so much anymore, and I realize I no longer feel the need to escape reality. I love this reality, this planet. Nothing artificial or manmade could rival the beauty of the real world. I enact a real story that happens right here, right now, in *this* place.

I no longer play a hero. I live as one.

Robots vs. Rewilding

Everyone knows that I hate robots. I have hated them for as long as I can remember. They give me the chills and cause me to go into fits of anger. I never really understood it. I guess I just chalked it up to them representing everything I hate about civilization: technology, control over life, consumerism, hipster-novelty...on and on.

At the Daft Punk Alive 2007 tour, standing in a crowd of people, facing a stage where two men danced in robot suits, in the middle of a giant pyramid, I realized just why I hate robots so much: they symbolize the future. I mean, obviously not the *actual* future, but civilization's *mythological* future. Etymonline.com describes the origin of *robot*:

> 1923, from English translation of 1920 play "R.U.R."
> ("Rossum's Universal Robots"), by Karel Čapek
> (1890–1938), from Czech robotnik "slave," from
> robota "forced labor, drudgery," from robotiti "to
> work, drudge," from an Old Czech source akin to
> Old Church Slavonic rabota "servitude," from rabu
> "slave" (see orphan), from a Slavic stem related to
> German Arbeit "work" (Old High German arabeit)

Robot means *slave*. Slaves occupy the bottom of a class system. A class system means hierarchy. Here we have Daft Punk, two guys dressed as robots standing inside a giant pyramid. Two symbols of hierarchy with tens of thousands of worshippers. Perhaps two wrongs make a right?

One classic motif of robot mythology that I find fascinating involves a robot seeking to feel human emotion. I can think of several examples: *Terminator 2* ("I know now why you cry"), *Short Circuit* ("Johnny-5 Alive!"), *Star Trek: The Next Generation* (Data's constant quest), the reimagined *Battlestar Galactica* (Cylons have feelings too), and *Electroma*, written and directed by Daft Punk about Daft Punk robots trying to become human. We can trace all of these back to Pinocchio, the marionette who wanted to live as a real boy. Perhaps the robot quest alludes to animist mythology, that even inanimate objects can have feelings. Or maybe the robot quest symbolizes the slave class of civilization trying to reclaim their humanity. But I have another theory.

The real myth of any robot quest looks like this: in the future robots will have feelings too. I identify several premises here. First, the future will have robots. Second, robots do not currently have feelings. This reflects two fundamental myths of civilization: that civilization will go on despite its inherent environmental destruction, and that other-than-humans (whether rocks, animals, plants, or wind) do not have feelings, do not have life, but like the robots we build, exist solely for our exploitation.

Now you might ask, "Why the hell would you, Urban Scout, go to a Daft Punk show?!? You hate robots! They give you the chills!" Well, you got me there. Despite their robot costumes and pyramids, I love their music and my friend got me in for free. Oh, the hypocrisy! I know. What can I say? I made the trip to Seattle from Portland to see these robots perform live, and what a show. I felt blown away by the amazing light show they put on.

In an interview called "Pyramid Schemers," Daft Punk's Thomas Bangalter says,

It's definitely fun to invent characters and to play around with them. It's almost this older concept of superheroes in comic books, where you have a line between fiction and reality, or between a regular and an animus character, and some kind of frantic image of another alter-ego—which are those robots.

I think a lot of the things we've been doing since we evolved into robots is really the concept of technology versus humanity. The science fiction is fun and entertaining, but in a very humble way this whole robot thing is only a metaphor for technology and its place today in the world, and in music. That's the whole idea behind the show.

In a funny way, the Daft Punk robots symbolize the exact opposite of what I do. They dress up like their vision of the future (the technological complexity of robots), and I dress up like my vision of the future (the technological simplicity and elegance of the hunter-gatherer). In my mind their future projection has no legs in the real world. It takes an industrial economy to build machines. It takes a civilization to have an industrial economy, and it takes agricultural practices to build a civilization. Since we know that agriculture destroys biodiversity, any sustainable future necessarily excludes robots.

I only hope that as time goes on, my work will inspire 10,000 people to come together to rewild and walk away from robots, pyramids, and slavery.

Superheroes vs. Rewilding

I often find myself rooting for the villains in the movies I watch these days. Most of civilization's superheroes act as police officers with special powers. Take Spider-Man: a cop who can climb buildings. Superman: a cop who can fly and shoot lasers out of his eyes. The Jedi: cops with glowing swords who can move things with their minds (no, they fight the Evil Empire, right? right?!). Batman: the vigilante guardian of civilization. They all succeed where the cops fail.

None of these heroes ever attack those who do the real damage: polluters, dictators, death squad soldiers, logging companies, dam builders, and a million other groups fucking up the planet. Okay, maybe Captain Planet. But how long did that lame show last? Who attacks those things in civilized mythology? The villains. Sometimes the villains just act as people even more power-hungry than those in power. These villains who want to "take over the world" only become villains because they have challenged the unspoken power relationship in civilization. You cannot do harm to those above you on the hierarchy. Even if you simply wish to climb the hierarchy. You must do it the way the state approves: through slave labor. Exploitation proves the only way to move up the pyramid, as moving up implies you stand above others.

The hero serves an important role in mythology. Our

heroes show us how to behave. In civilized context, they show us "right" and "wrong" with their actions. They teach us to protect and serve civilization, specifically the rich and powerful. So what does a rewilding, anti-civilization hero look like?

I like the villains who just want to tear the whole system down. Like Batman's arch-nemesis, the Joker. And of course, no other historical or mythological figure makes guerrilla warfare look cooler than Robin Hood. Living in the wild and stealing from the rich to give to the poor? If only Robin Hood and the Joker could join forces!

A rewilding hero would stand as a "bioregional patriot." They would move us from the paradigm of identification with a nation, with civilization, to identification with the land. People who protect and serve the land they live on, outside of civilization's control. Living in and with the wilds, pushing the rewild frontier in on civilization. While those in urban environments experience the worst of a collapsing monolith, those out in the wild will live freer lives, just as Robin Hood did. For rewilding to catch on, we need role models. We need heroes. Real or imagined. And we need them now.

Ageism vs. Rewilding

In our culture, the young and the elderly receive the worst prejudice and abuse. We force children into schooling where the system coerces them to do what those in power tell them. Then when people reach a certain age they get dumped into nursing homes and forgotten. Oppression of the young and old happens so consistently it looks normal to us, and most people don't see it as oppression. In fact most people don't see it at all. As you age you see a positive progression up the hierarchy. As an adult you forget the oppression suffered as a child while accepting the benefits that come with growing older. Once you reach a certain age, people no longer perceive you as "productive" or "useful," and once again you plummet to the bottom of the pyramid.

Civilizationists like to project hierarchy onto nonhier-archical structures. This happens when we look at an indigenous culture's system of information dispersal and transformation. One of the elements of culture commonly discussed in rewilding involves the notion of "elders," specifically their purpose in an indigenous context. The concept of elders has not evaded civilized cultures en-tirely, although civilized "elders" transmit a very different structure than those of indigenous peoples.

In indigenous cultures, elders help keep their commu-nities intact by teaching the young about the ways of nature. We know that a tactic of white civilizationists, used to assimilate Native Americans, involved estranging the young from their elders. An elder from a native's perspective does not look like someone with generic "wisdom" but someone with a special kind of wisdom that relates to living closely with their particular landbase.

To call an elder simply *an old person with wisdom* does little justice to the wisdom traditional elders actually hold about their place. "Wisdom" varies from worldview to worldview. In a world based on direct experiences in a particular landbase, elders would have logged the most time observing that land. It makes sense that they would hold the key to cultural transmission. Elders occur more organically in that kind of system. They do not force their knowledge or perception of the land on younger people. The younger people recognize that these older people can give them insights into how to live on that particular piece of land, in that particular way. In a culture that continually destroys its landbase, we can rest assured that our "elders" have no land-based wisdom. Noticing that the elderly people in civilization do not have special, landbase-wise qualities, and do not act as keepers of a sustainable culture, some people have made the distinction between these civilized *olders* and native *elders*.

I find it funny when older people use the phrase, "You act childish." Children have a nature of their own, for sure, but mostly they mimic the adults and culture around them. So they act out how they see their parents act. They reenact their parents. Therefore children don't act childish, they act adultish. And as American children have proven time and time again, most adults act like crazy, controlling assholes.

I have seen many wilderness-style programs mistakenly refer to elders as "the over fifty crowd," as though the age of fifty signifies something. Perhaps in real, intact indigenous cultures the elders have aged over fifty years, but this distinction does not apply to civilization's olders. What happens when you take a bunch of crazy, controlling, asshole-ish olders and tell them they need to live as elders? All hell breaks loose. I have noticed that within a culture based on domination it seems all too easy to simply project domination onto an egalitarian system and call it egalitarian. This methodology has spawned many vampiric olders who seek nothing but a power-over relationship with youth, which I have experienced firsthand. Without fully articulating an elder's social position, we see a bunch of olders who now think of themselves as elders. I only know one word to describe such a person: fraudulent.

It seems many older people feel entitled to praise and respect from youth, despite their potential lack of experience or wisdom. I see olders adultishly attempt to assert themselves as elders the way nerdy children in middle school flounder while trying to act "cool" (myself included there). Rather than have comfort with themselves, olders want to have something they don't. They can fake it for a while, but eventually the younger people expose the deception by the olders and take their friendship away. Rich, childless olders seem the most common. They can't even hold a conversation with a younger person without pointing out their age. To olders, people within a domination-based civilization, an elder looks like someone in a position of power. Power the older never had. And when young people buy into that...disaster ensues.

We define both olders and elders by age and yet age does not indicate experience. Experience indicates experience. Age *relates* to experience because the more you age, the more experience you have. However, the kinds of experiences you have determine what you know, how you know, and what you have learned from your experience.

A particular set of experiences gives someone a particular kind of wisdom.

Experience forms the foundation of wisdom, and indigenous cultures worked well at regulating experiences through yearly rituals. It makes sense that they would have a group of people who had reached a certain age and gone through all the same rituals and rites and shared similar experiences that the youth had yet to go through. The group we refer to as elders became members of that group not because they aged, but because they went through similar rituals together on a particular piece of land and undertook the facilitation of those rituals on behalf of younger people.

If we understand that an elder means someone who has gone through many rites and rituals, it makes sense that they would know and feel things beyond our recognition. Civilization breeds experiences that destroy our relationship to the land. While a high school diploma may serve as a rite to many of us, how many high school graduates know how to live sustainably? How many indigenous eighteen-year-olds do? Civilization's elders, or olders, carry the wisdom of denial, distraction, and escapism.

If we see how age creates an elder in this kind of indigenous culture, and how age relates to power within civilization, we can easily see how a civilized person would project their worldview onto another. The term *elder* does not allude to an unarticulated hierarchical structure, at the top of which elders sit. If elders get some sort of special treatment, it involves their dependency on the younger. I don't get an elder a plate of food because they have a special status in a hierarchy but because they have trouble walking. It almost seems as if their powerlessness in physicality has given them power in sociality or spirituality. This leads to another quality of an elder:

humility. It seems that elders carry humility, not only because of years of learning from nature but also because, like children, they require help from people stronger and healthier than they.

If *elder* refers to someone with humility who has gone through experiences I want to go through, who has rewilded in my particular bioregion and has wisdom of living with it over a long period of time, well...none exist. Not within my culture anyway. Bits and pieces of wisdom exist here and there in different native people and in books. I use those to cobble together my future. This shows another example the importance of honoring living native communities and allying with them. Perhaps someday we'll have elders again, but it will probably happen without anyone noticing the change. The key to having a successful culture does not involve mimicking what we see natives doing, but truly understanding how their cultures function. A highly functional culture produces elders who teach the young how to have a highly functional culture. In a culture without elders, rewilding humans need not try to act like them. We need to learn how to live with the land. Those who experiment in living with the land, regardless of their age, reveal the people that I have something to learn from. And when these people have aged with the land and gained much knowledge and experience, young people will naturally want to know how to follow in their footsteps.

School vs. Rewilding

Indigenous cultures do not have schools. In fact in three million years of human history, we've only had schools for a few hundred. What does that tell you? People did fine without schools, lived sustainably without schools. In spite of all its rhetoric of education, civilization continues to destroy the planet at an accelerating rate. Not only did we do fine without schools, we did better.

I always hated school. No wait, I mean, I always *fucking* hated school. In fact I dropped out five times from four schools. Four of the programs I actually chose to go into myself. The fifth, compulsory schooling, no one ever gave me a choice. As soon as I realized I had a choice, I left.

Even those who claim to have loved school can't possibly honestly mean it. My friend Willem loves it when people say, "I liked school." He simply replies, "So you stayed inside and cried during all of your snow days?" Unless they liked school in the Stockholm syndrome sense (also called trauma-bonding), in which people become sympathetic and loyal to their captors or abusers.

Schooling not only destroys our passion for life, it also never allows us to know it exists. As children we have no choice but to place trust in our culture to meet our needs. We do what it dictates, expecting to learn how to live in the world. Placed in school, with a one-size-fits-all curriculum, we do not learn to follow the things in life that interest us and give us power as individuals. The hierarchy of school falls into place quite easily because some kids do really well in school. This puts all the kids who don't do well lower on the pyramid. Of course the ones who do well in school enjoy it because they reap the benefits of sitting higher on the hierarchy. Those who do what teachers ask of them (homework, raising their hand to speak, asking to use the restroom), those who have no difficulty tossing out their individuality—their soul—reap the benefits: pizza parties, good grades, honor role, the elitism and pride that come from thinking you have more smarts than your fellow classmates.

I hated school. But that doesn't mean that I hated all of my teachers. On the contrary, I think that teachers themselves simply serve as captives of a larger system. I had some really great teachers who shaped my life, and some real assholes too. Most teachers don't realize this and think they can change the system or work the system. Unfortunately the system itself does the teaching, and you cannot change a flawed system. It doesn't matter what subjects you learn or teach, the system (or structure) teaches you the real lessons: watch the clock, follow instructions, fear those in power and your peers, and understand that those in power determine your intelligence and self-worth.

In elementary school my teachers loved me. They raved to my parents about my creativity and imagination. They placed me in the TAG (Talented and Gifted) program in kindergarten. I believed I had more smarts than those not in the program because I had more "talent" and more "gifts," which led to an elitist attitude. Conversely, those who didn't go to TAG felt like they did not have the same intelligence, which filled them with self-loathing.

In my first year of middle school I attended Outdoor School, a public school program for children to learn about nature. By the time I went to Outdoor School I had participated in Boy Scouts for about one year. At my Boy Scout camps I could wander off for hours into the woods as long as I had a buddy, a watch, a compass, and told people which direction I started in and when I planned to arrive back in camp. This allowed all the freedom a young child could ask to explore the beauty of nature without interference. We could simply experience nature without any *civilized agenda*. This made me hate Outdoor School. We couldn't leave the sight of an adult and had to constantly take notes in a mindless, boring way with industrial-made instruments. How do you make the natural world totally fucking boring and alienating? Projectile vomit the compulsory schooling structure onto it, and voila: Outdoor School. Of course, the only way you could get funding to put school kids outside at all would involve tainting the experience through the same old schooling process.

All week the counselors spoke of a "Plant Village" that we would experience on Thursday. They really built it up. All week we heard the hype. I remember thinking at twelve years old, "Hell, with all this hype, at least Plant Village will be pretty cool." On the long-anticipated morning of Plant Village, we met in a large circle. It went something like this:

> **Counselor:** All right, now the moment you've waited all week for... Does everyone feel ready for PLANT VILLAGE?!?
> **Campers:** YEEEEEEEAAAAHHHH!!!
> **Counselor:** Awesome! You won't believe your eyes when you see it!
> *(pause)*
> **Counselor:** But! Before we go to plant village we've selected a *special* group of kids who get to

go on a special, *super cool* hike to an old growth forest... instead!

(Pause... all the kids look around confused. I think to myself, "Why the hell would anyone want to go to an old growth forest after all this hype over plant village?")

Counselor: Okay, if I read out your name come stand over here.

The counselor began to call out names. The first three names called belonged to the three loudest *African American* kids in my class, and it became painfully obvious what the teachers had done (not to mention the unarticulated connection between class and race and hierarchy). They dreamed up this bullshit hike in order to get the "troublemakers" as far away from Plant Village as possible so that it would run smoothly. Then they called a few other names of some obnoxious white kids, and it confirmed my theory. I felt so embarrassed for those kids. Then the most shocking, transformative, eye-opening thing happened to me: *they called my fucking name!*

The psychological pain felt intense. This story still makes me tear up with rage as I recall it. I couldn't quite talk at first. I felt winded. "*Am* I a troublemaker?" I thought in B-English. "They think I *am* a troublemaker?" This confused me all to hell. Just a year before, my teachers thought of me as the clever, creative genius. I remember thinking, "Oh. You think I belong with the troublemakers? Okay. Fine. I'll give you what you want. *I'll make some fucking trouble.*" I looked at Marcus, someone who acted like such an asshole to me (threatening me with a knife several times that year), and for the first time I felt such sympathy towards him and all the others in this group. I got it. If they had mislabeled me, they had mislabeled all of us, and in doing so gave us permission to make trouble. If those in power tell you what you "are," then you must give them what they want. At that point I stopped doing homework and completely lost interest in school. I didn't really do much "troublemaking" because I didn't have the energy for it. I fell into a suicidal depression that year that lasted until I transferred to an alternative arts high school for my sophomore year (which I later dropped out of).

I never fucking asked about Plant Village, but it probably sucked balls.

Because of my decline in interest, my freshman year of high school the counselors placed me in "intermediate math," aka math for allegedly not-so-smart kids. I had the wits to read through the lines and see the hierarchy of "intelligence": Advanced Math (smart kids), Algebra 1 (normal kids), and Intermediate Math (dumb kids). Of course, none of the kids in any of those classes had more smarts than anyone else; these classes merely reflected the arbitrary one-size-fits-all curriculum. I demanded my counselor change me to normal math. But the time I spent in intermediate math made me realize that those kids had about as much interest in school as I did, and it had nothing to do with their actual intelligence.

By experiencing the full spectrum of the intellectual hierarchy, from smart TAG kid to stupid math kid, I understood the hierarchy in a way none of my peers did. Especially because I fell down the ladder of hierarchy rather than climbing it. I lost benefits and saw the results instead of gaining benefits and losing sight of previous psychological abuse. Those who do well all through school or those who do better later do not see or forget what it feels like to sit at the bottom. While those who suffer at the bottom, like cattle raised in cages for meat, never get a taste of the benefits; they don't know anything better.

Looking back now, I can't imagine a better way of killing the souls of children and preparing them for slavery. It looks rather genius and sinister, and it should. The same great minds who facilitated the Great Depression and the creation of the Federal Reserve—J. P. Morgan, Rockefeller, Woodrow Wilson, and others—brought us compulsory schooling because, as Woodrow Wilson said, "We want one class to have a liberal education. We want another class, a very much larger class of necessity, to forgo the privilege of a liberal education and fit themselves to perform specific difficult manual tasks." The first class, who would receive "a liberal education," obviously included the rich, those who at the time attended private colleges (before they came up with the genius idea of trapping poor people in debt by enticing them to pay for this "liberal education").

By dropping out of high school (to teach myself wilderness survival), I faced the wrath of mythology pertaining to "drop-outs": having to flip burgers and pump gas for the rest of my life. Funny, in the real world you realize just how much a high school diploma, and yes, even a college degree, will get you: not a damn thing but thousands of dollars in debt. From age sixteen to nineteen, I worked at coffee shops as the youngest employee with no "education." I made the same amount and performed the same tasks as the twenty- to thirty-somethings who all held not just high school diplomas but college degrees as well.

In a hierarchical economy, only a few people actually work the job they wanted, and only a few get paid to do what they went to school for. But more importantly, to work at the bottom of the pyramid, you don't have to have shit for a degree, and since most people get degrees these days (or try) it means a whole lot of slaves in a whole lot of debt, just to have a piece of paper that they didn't need to work the job they do. The only perk the piece of paper has amounts to the feeling of self-satisfaction for having attained the paper. Anyway, if you think you need a degree to get a job, you can always just lie. I've never heard of anyone actually checking.

The smugness with which many high school and college grads refer to their "education" makes me want to vomit. Most people get what they call an education, and yet they don't even know anything about reality. I mean, about the physical reality of this planet and its workings and its other-than-human community. For example, how many people, specifically urban people, know five native plants? Their medicinal uses? How to process them to make them most effective? We have no knowledge of self-sufficiency outside of civilization's economy. We do not know how to get food, except from the handouts of our masters as we perform physical and psychological slavery while exploiting the planet for them. If forced schooling didn't fuck you up enough, how about making you pay to have your mind inculcated into a civilized paradigm, then believing it made you all the better?

College strengthens our resolve in hierarchical structures by making us invest finances in civilized mythology. As children we never really had a choice: our parents made us go to school. Later in life they made us choose (and pay) to go, further solidifying our belief in these systems. This only deepens the denial of college grads; if we spent all that time and money for nothing, we would have to face the reality of our way of life and admit that civilization duped us.

You only need a resume for one reason: to work for someone you don't know. All my life in school we learn that we need to have a diploma so that we can write it on our resume. But why do we need a resume? What does a degree really mean? If you have a large social network, you don't need a resume because people know you and they know what qualifies you to have a particular job. You don't need a resume to start your own business. You don't need degrees to start your own business. A resume stands in for lack of relationships with people. A degree says, you don't know this person, but they have had this particular training that you believe qualifies them for this job. Again, you can always lie. I—and nearly everyone I have spoken to—have lied plenty of times! To live as an entrepreneur, you simply need *street cred.* We all know that most of the things we learn in school we won't use or we forget after the test. This means that if you actually have earned street cred, you did so through using information (meaning you won't forget it because it has a purpose beyond an arbitrary test) and doing things you'll continue to do.

Just because the system of schooling further ingrains our dependency on the hierarchy doesn't mean you can't derive value from schooling; it just comes at the cost of training your brain in a systemic way. We need a new system of education that works against hierarchy, against creating slaves dependent on the system to provide their needs in exchange for painfully laborious, soul-sucking work.

We need to rewild the way we see education. *School ≠ education.* I can hear you say, but what about schools that teach rewilding skills? If I want to live as a hunter-gather and have no need for money, then spending time running classes to get money looks hypocritical. What if I spent that time hunting and gathering with friends instead? Then I wouldn't need money. It works as a paradox. Of course, we all have to start somewhere, and the schools that teach rewilding skills work as a great place to meet people interested in rewilding. This paradox can do more harm than good if you get caught in its pitfalls.

I have noticed that many students of these programs (myself included at one time) become dependent on them. Rather than seeking out relationships with people who practice rewilding near our homes, we pay people money to teach us, without having to build a relationship with them. It doesn't help you build a relationship that will last. These schools don't build friendships, or culture, which works as the real teacher. You still pay the person money to hang out with them.

I often justify teaching rewilding skills for money as a means of escaping wage slavery. And yet I have come across many rewilding programs that can never make that much money, so you spend so much time trying to get students and marketing your classes that you don't have much time for hunting and gathering. Again, it becomes a paradox.

Not everyone wants a community. Some people want to learn these skills and take them back to their community, and that works well for people like me who love to teach but feel a little guilty and lame for not spending more time working on building my own community. If I can help individual communities by exchanging my skills for some cash, I feel no guilt. This shows the real value in schools. A community with no skills sends a member to go learn them at a school and return to share them.

At a seven-day primitive skills school I went to, the celebrity teacher told everyone that if they couldn't survive it meant their "skills sucked." That kind of attitude can make you feel guilty about not living 100% wild. Fuck that. We don't have a wild culture to provide for us for twelve years while we learn to rewild, and we don't have time to feel guilty about it. But we do have modern technology and resources that we can leverage to our benefit. We can use them to replicate the support of the culture we don't have, while we build it.

This school also claimed that you would have all the skills to "survive lavishly" by the end of the week. A nice fantasy, but in reality you cannot learn to rewild in seven days. I find it funny when I ask Joe Blow if he thinks he could survive the collapse of civilization and he says, "No problem." Of all the time I have spent rewilding, I would never make such a claim. At this point I don't really concern myself with surviving the collapse as much as I feel concerned with breaking out of the prison of civilization. Indigenous peoples don't "survive in the woods." They practice ancient, streamlined, seasonal routines that provided comfort, enjoyment, and sustainability. Because of their routines they live(d) in an environment *teeming* with wild foods now decimated by civilization. So tell me, if civilization collapsed tonight, could you live that way tomorrow? The next day? Six months from now? Five years from now? Five hundred years from now? How long does it take to build that kind of culture? How long did it take to build the Amazon? How long does it take to die of thirst or hypothermia or the flu (without antibiotics)? How many people could our ravaged lands support? Would you still answer, "No problem?"

I appreciate these programs, workshops, and schools for what they teach, but I believe you can't really learn or truly know something by reading about it in a book or listening about it at a lecture at a school. I like to use the example of learning foreign languages. You can learn it in a class or you can immerse yourself in a place where you can only speak the one language. I can take classes or read books about participating in nature, or I can go out and immerse myself in a primitive lifestyle. Similarly, most Americans learn Spanish with the intent to *visit* Mexico, but how many of them learn Spanish so they can *move* to Mexico? I believe rewilding means *moving to Mexico*, so to speak. We need to create rewilding cultures immersion-style.

By using these civilized forms of information hoarding, rewilding skills remain under lock and key by forcing people to participate in the economy of civilization for access to the information, while continuing to spread the alienation and lack of culture that promotes this way of life. As long as this remains true, we will never have what it takes to form these rewilding cultures. I do not mean to devalue schools that teach rewilding skills, I only point out that if you use money in place of real relationships, civilization owns you. Schools that teach rewilding can work as a great first step, but if we yearn to move beyond civilization and truly rewild, if we wish to get the knowledge that will allow us to unlock the food, we must work to unlock the knowledge and skills of rewilding. We need to change our strategies for sharing this information.

Current strategies

The field guide, web information

Books cost money. Some may perceive this as trading and not as hoarding: exchanging money for information. Information stored in books generally remains under lock and key. In a field guide, the knowledge of skills remains locked in a book. Copyright laws prohibit an individual from dispersing the information. Also, books seal information in a fixed state; once written down, the information cannot change. This makes books themselves a kind of false guide, as rewilding bases itself on an ever-changing landscape.

Primitive skills schools

By their nature, schools form hierarchical relationships. Information flows one way, from the minority (of instructors) to the majority (of students). By paying an "expert" to teach you about skills, or as an instructor, you become obligated to give the students their "money's worth." Information at primitive schools remains under lock and key. In order for primitive skills schools to stay in business, free access to primitive skills information and communities must not exist. The schools themselves represent the lock and money represents the key to this knowledge. Ideologically those who start wilderness schools generally don't have the intention of training people to rewild.

Primitive skills rendezvous

The rendezvous represents the closest format of information sharing to Open Space Technology. You must pay money to attend, and you must seek the approval of the organizers in order to hold a class. Some rendezvous do not cost money and some do.

Emphasis on artifacts

Most of these sources emphasize physical skills and crafts such as flint-knapping, basketry, and hide tanning. How many "primitive skills" books, schools, and rendezvous teach invisible social technologies such as childrearing, storytelling, clear communication, group meetings, oral ecology, hunter-gatherer land management practices, etc.? Not many.

Unlocking rewilding knowledge

Community-building skill-shares

By running a public skill-share (such as a rewild camp) you can attract more people to rewilding and promote awareness for it while learning skills from others in the community. You can also run a private skill-share for family and friends. The purpose of the skill-share comes back to the idea of building relationships and forming real cultures that hunt and gather together. I believe in exchanges and trading, and the skill-share does exactly that. You share your skills and learn from others who share theirs. You exchange your talents and knowledge instead of money.

If we wish to unlock the food, but in order to do that we must first have the knowledge of how to procure food, it follows that we must unlock this information. Rewild.info and community-building skill-shares attempt to make the primitive skills school, field guide, and old-school rendezvous nearly obsolete (in terms of function). I believe it would behoove us to borrow the hacker philosophy of freedom of information and start spreading it as fast as we can.

Voting vs. Rewilding

Voting—the last bastion of mind control that civilization holds over many of us anti-civilizationists. I mean, why not vote? Just scribble in a few bubbles and drop the paper in a box. Voting can't hurt, right? ...Wrong!

We all know, even those of us who continue to vote, that voting does not change anything. It merely absorbs your energy and keeps you psychologically invested in the outcome of a broken system that your vote cannot fix. Voting works as another form of denial: believing that we can have a quick fix. Denial that if we just change people, not the system itself, things will work out. Even though we all know things won't change much.

Now, you may say, "If it doesn't really matter, who cares if I vote or not?"

Like telling Canadians to vote in the American election, rewilding involves the creation of a new system. We don't want to change the leaders of our culture, we want to create a new culture altogether. By voting you only prove that you still have a psychological investment in denial. The idea that it doesn't matter, doesn't mean, "So do it anyway." It takes time to think about who to vote for, what laws to vote for, and then the disappointment and heartache you feel the day of the election when even though the dipshit you voted for wins the popular vote, some other asshole steals the election anyway. WTF? Voting takes a lot more energy and investment than filling out a sheet of paper and dropping it in a slot. That investment of your energy goes right to the evildoers of civilization. "Ha ha! We got them to vote another time!"

"I'll stop voting when I have a feral culture to join." This argument for voting makes more sense to me. And yet, to that I would respond: only one way exists to create a feral culture, and that involves walking away from civilization. We can have a foot in both worlds, sure, but voting doesn't show your active involvement in lessening damage (voting for the lesser of two evils), it merely shows you still want to remain in denial. Walk away. Walk away. Let it go.

Of course, we also hear that real change doesn't happen with voting in politics but when we "vote with our dollars." Fuck that. "Voting with dollars" means the same thing as voting: investing in civilization. Whether physically with money or psychologically with a ballot. Buying "green" light bulbs will not save the planet, and the more time we spend believing that technology will save us rather than learning to abandon those technologies, the more time we commit to destroying the planet.

One may argue that one leader will do "less damage" than another, but it comes back to your investment of energy. When you vote, you feed the system. Deciding who to vote for, reading up on issues, and all that crap takes time away from rewilding and programs your brain to actually care about the outcome. When the bigger asshole wins (or more accurately steals) the election, you find yourself caring a lot. And for what?

Now I like the idea of the slogan "Vote with bullets, not ballots," because it brings more attention to how real change could come about: by eliminating the state's monopoly on violence and allowing people, local communities to choose how to behave. Though I still think "Vote with bullets, not ballots" implies revolution within the hierarchy, not the dismantling of it, because hey, if you still think in terms of voting, you still think in terms of changing the system. Whether you vote with ballots or bullets, the system remains.

Now I could say, "Vote with your feet and walk away," but by using the term *vote*, we still operate on the language (and therefore culture) of the abuser. I think saying, "Don't vote, walk away," sounds more like a cowardly hunger strike. "I'll walk away until you decide to change your ways!" It makes no sense either. Don't vote at all.

Now comes the part where I tell you that I actually do vote, and no, not just in *Dancing with the Stars* and myspace polls, but yes, I admit that despite everything I just said, I vote in politics too! Well, sort of. I vote for local issues that will protect wild areas. I vote for schools to receive less money (*fuck 'em*). I vote for the lesser of two evils because I know that a third party will not change the system any more than my lesser evil, but at least we can do lesser evil, while in the meantime we continue to dismantle civilization and rewild.

I guess it comes down to knowing that investing your time and energy in voting means remaining in denial that voting doesn't matter, and thinking that civilization will change. It doesn't look like denial as long as you know that voting may (but most likely will not) protect the environment for a bit longer and that we need to spend more time dismantling civilization than volunteering for a political campaign (NADER 2000, yo!).

Bureaucracy vs. Rewilding

Federal officials have called for killing about 30 sea lions near Bonneville Dam each year to keep them from gobbling a rising share of Northwest salmon that the government spends millions of dollars to protect.

— The Oregonian, January 18, 2008

Dear salmon. I have a confession to make. While working as a production assistant for television commercials, a friend called me for a job...on a political campaign advertisement.

The conversation went like this:

> "Hey, Peter. I've got a job for you if you want it."
> "Yeah, sure. I need some work right now."
> "Great. Well, how do you feel about political ads?"
> I think for a second and ask, "Does the person belong to the Democratic or Republican party?"
> He pauses. "Does it matter?"
> I laugh. "...Nope."
> "Let's just say the guy doesn't look pretty."

The job felt about as horrible as you might imagine. We drove around the state for two days shooting the local political candidate (some billionaire business tycoon) "talk" with "people" about issues. Of course, he didn't really talk about anything because the footage would serve as B-roll for the voiceover and text that would narrate the commercial. We drove to Molalla where he had some farmer buddies to show him talking with farmers. We went to a shipping room for one of his business clients to show that he cares about businesses (that business happened to have all kinds of plaques on the wall in honor of their donations to anti-abortion organizations).

At lunch the topic of politics came up. Some people agreed that Al Gore lost the election because his posture felt too stiff. I wanted to say, "Actually, he won the election. Bush stole it, remember?" But then I remembered that I didn't give a shit who "won" or stole anything. It all looks like a sham to me anyway (I voted for Nader, ha!). I had worked on many commercials at this point. Never had the crew eaten in complete silence like this, with only an occasional glance of recognition between us to acknowledge that the people talking sounded insane.

As the tension built on that shoot, things just grew more and more sinister. We traveled to the political candidate's mansion for the last location for the shoot. His backyard had a vineyard that ended at his own personal dock on the Willamette River in yuppieville Lake Oswego. When we got to the house he said, "I really only intended it to reach 4,000 square feet, but I just couldn't stop building! (*Yuck yuck!*) All together now I think it stands at 11,000 square feet."

Out back we set up some gear for the shoot on his dock. Two of his fishing buddies showed up for part of the video of him talking with fishermen. The producer felt like they needed a third person, so he hired an old Asian man with a long white beard who had coincidentally come to the house to clean the guy's pool.

Down on the dock, tensions grew. Not just because the sun would soon set and we raced the daylight, but because of all the bullshit we had seen and experienced in the previous hours. They began shooting B-roll of the political candidate talking to the fishermen. The director suggested the man talk about fishing policy, even though they wouldn't actually record it, just to "set the mood." So off he went. He began by saying that the endangered sea lions who hunt the salmon held the responsibility for the depleted runs of salmon. He suggested killing sea lions, *endangered sea lions*, as a solution to declining salmon populations. He argued that environmentalists, by protecting sea lions, indirectly held responsibility for declining salmon populations.

Wait a minute. We all know that dams kill salmon by not letting salmon return to their spawning grounds. A few years (depending on the life span of the particular salmon) without a fish ladder and you have no more salmon runs upriver from the dam. Dams killed the salmon. We all know that logging killed the eggs of those salmon who did make it past the dams by silt run-off from clear-cuts burying the eggs and by removing trees that shaded the river, making it hotter than the temperature that salmon eggs need to mature. We know that those salmon who survived to make it back out to the ocean died in fishing nets from commercial fishing companies.

At that point I turned away from the crew and started to cry. I thought about a discussion I had with Derrick Jensen. He said that when you kill something you make an agreement that you will take responsibility for the continuation of that species. This political commercial paid me $200 a day for two days, a grand total of $400. During the Nuremberg trials, they sentenced Julius Streicher, editor of the weekly Nazi newspaper, to death. What about the writers of the paper? What about the paper boys (and girls)? They all played a part as good Germans. I stood on that dock, keeping my mouth shut and playing the part of the good civilian.

I couldn't escape the fact that in some way, my work contributed to the success of bullshit politicians and the continuation of a civilized system of programmed environmental devastation. Whether Republican or Democrat, whether the guy won the election or not. The simple fact that two years later "federal officials" have called for the death of sea lions shows that it doesn't matter which person takes office: the momentum of civilization's destruction always wins out.

I knelt down and looked into the murky waters of the Willamette, wiping the tears from my eyes. I began speaking to the salmon. "I promise you, I will do whatever I can, use the tools I have, to help your species survive. Please hold on. Please."

A few weeks earlier another article came out about the death of salmon at the hands of the good citizens.

> Salmon survived massive dams and fishing fleets, but now they're feeling the heat of global warming—and it's likely to hammer them as hard as anything they've faced.
>
> — *The Oregonian*, January 6, 2008

Salmon did not survive the dams and fishing fleets, as the moronic *Oregonian* notes. An endangered species looks more like someone who has cancer: you don't know if they will survive or not. The salmon populations would not have declined to near extinction without the logging and dams and overfishing.

I have a genius idea. Let's pour thousands of tons of concrete across a river and stop the fish who spawn in it from having the ability to come back next year. After a few years, most will no longer live. Dams (a product of civilization) decimated the salmon. Logging (a product of civilization) kicked them while they lay on the ground. And now, mysterious global warming (influenced heavily by civilization) lifts a club to the sky threatening the final blow and taking credit away from civilized dams and logging. How convenient for the hydro-timber industries. Then when fishermen complain, we blame the deaths of the salmon on the endangered sea lions (who became endangered when the dams killed their main food supply, the salmon) and kill them. Who fucking came up with this idea? No, seriously. Who fucking came up with this shit?!?

Humans lived in the northwest coast of this continent for (at least) 8,000 years in a sustainable manner as hunter-gatherer-horticulturalists. Civilization has occupied (after stealing) this land for a mere 200 years. How many more do you think it will take to destroy every life here? How long do you think before civilization puts humans on the endangered species list? Do you honestly think corporations will allow the government (with all its bullshit laws and loopholes) to dismantle the dams?

How long before the rest of the oceans have no more life in them? Oh yeah...forty years.

> Unless humans act now, seafood may disappear by 2048, concludes the lead author of a new study that paints a grim picture for ocean and human health.
>
> — *National Geographic*, November 2, 2006

I saw a wanted poster with a fish on it on a paper in a rack at my favorite taco joint and had to pick it up. It made me so fucking angry, as papers do (which shows you why I don't read them), that I had to rewrite the article here for you to see, along with my commentary. The title of the article? "Wanted Dead or Alive: The Pikeminnow."

> Ravenous trash fish prey on baby salmon. Traps don't work. Poison doesn't work. It's up to the Bounty Hunters.

Okay, you had me at "ravenous trash fish," hook, line, and sinker.

> On a recent cloudy Friday, perched in a black low-slung fishing boat stained by guts and bait, Nikolay Zaremskiy pulled a steady stream of money from the Columbia River in the form of muscular, slimy bills.
>
> These wriggling prizes are not the usual stuff of anglers' daydreams—rainbow trout or glittering steelhead. Far from it. These are northern pikeminnows, ravenous predators that prey on helpless young salmon smolt as they migrate downstream from their spawning grounds to the Pacific.

"Ravenous predators." Right off the bat we have this statement made twice already. Maybe if the writer says it over and over again it will make it true. They don't even try to hide their propaganda anymore. Well, shit. They don't even have to. Most of the stupid fucks out there read that and think, "Those fucking ravenous fish! Let's fucking kill them all!"

> Pikeminnows devour millions of salmon and steelhead every year. So voracious is their appetite,

> in fact, that experts think they kill as many as all
> the Columbia River's massive hydroelectric dams
> combined.

What the fuck. Read that a few times. Can you see the irony there? The dams kill millions of salmon every year. They said it, not me. And yet, who takes the wrap? First the sea lions, now the pikeminnow!?! Anyone but us! I love how "experts" think that. What experts? Who "thinks" that? I "think" a lot of things. Not all of them stand true. Okay, but get this:

> Pikeminnows thrive in reservoirs, so the construc-
> tion of hydroelectric dams on the Columbia River
> triggered a massive increase in population.

So you admit the pikeminnow "problem" wouldn't exist if the dams didn't exist? So not only do the dams themselves kill "millions of salmon," but their mere existence creates habitat for one of the salmon's natural predators to kill "millions" more. And as a response, civ blames the fish?...Uh, cool. Oh snap, check out this editorial response from the *Pikeminnows Weekly*:

> Civilizationists devour millions of salmon and
> steelhead every year. So voracious is their ap-
> petite, in fact, that expert pikeminnows think they
> kill as many as all we pikeminnows eat! Yeah,
> and they call us ravenous predators! Ha! They
> brought the salmon populations down to only 1%
> from where they stood 100 years ago, and created
> the perfect habitat for our species...And now they
> want to call us ravenous predators?!! FUCK YOU,
> CIVILIZATIONISTS! You made us! Your dams
> killed the salmon! You did this! YOU!!!!

Yeah. I totally agree with that pikeminnow. Fuck you guys. Back to the terrible article:

> In an effort to put a lid on this relentless slaughter, the Pacific States Marine Fisheries Commission has tried methods from trapping to netting—and even considered poison. None of it seemed like a good fix.

"Relentless slaughter." I seriously didn't make this up. These people are fucking insane. Just fucking insane. Just. Remove. The. Fucking. Dams.

> In the end, the agency settled on a time-tested approach from the outlaw days of the Old West. Declaring the species a menace to society it put a bounty on the fish's head, attracting a small but ruthless armada of anglers like Zaremskiy who share a single passion—preying on the predator at eight bucks a pop.

I declare that this civilization stands as a menace to all species. In response I say we hire Nature's Bounty Hunters, those who work for the bounty of nature itself to do some real work around here. According to the rest of this fish-hate piece of propaganda, this guy has made $50,000 so far this season and "will single-handedly save at least 160,000 salmon from being swallowed into oblivion."

In order for the salmon to survive they need to make it to the ocean, and back up the river to spawn when they mature. The dams need to go. In order for salmon to spawn they need cool and silt-free places to do so. Logging needs to stop. In order for the mature salmon to make it back to the ocean, we need commercial fishing to stop. The amount of paperwork and lobbying and funding and time needed to do that adds up to an impossibility. It feels hard enough just to get a couple of friends to agree on what movie to go see. Bureaucratic means will not save the salmon. They take too long and the salmon don't have the time. A marine biologist in *The Oregonian* actually gave the best (and possibly only) way to save the salmon:

> "We want to be very careful to be very sure we are removing the right animals," said Garth Griffin, a marine biologist with the fisheries service in Portland.
>
> — *The Oregonian*, January 18, 2008

Don't you find it funny that I actually agree with this biologist!? I think we need to think very carefully and make sure we remove the right animals. If by removing the "right" animals they mean removing those animals who destroy the most salmon and by removing them we will see the most impact on improving the restoration of salmon populations. Following this line of thinking...sea lions don't come to my mind when I think about the "right" animals to remove.

I have a better idea. How about people dismantle thirty of the real salmon gobblers, the dams, logging and fishing industries, every year? Thirty of those salmon gobblers a year. Of course, this may prove difficult to use bureaucratic means...We'll have to think up some new ideas, outside of civilization's box...if you know what I mean. I wonder how many more salmon you could save by taking that fifty grand and investing it in a few well-placed explosives?

Say it with me:

CIVILIZATION OUT OF CASCADIA NOW!

Fuck it. CIVILIZATION OUT OF THIS PLANET NOW!

Ethics vs. Rewilding

Since its inception, civilization has created a value system of good vs. evil. The concept of good and evil (or the more scientific "right" and "wrong") seems to permeate much of our thought and actions, and we have projected this concept onto indigenous mythologies as well. "Surely the notion of good and evil comes from human nature, not culture!" But if we look deeper, we see that this notion lives and dies with a culture of destruction.

Some people think the Pope creates good. Some people think the Pope creates evil. Good and evil exist as subjective, cultural perspectives. Some believe that clear-cutting forests creates good by providing people with jobs and lumber. Others say that clear-cutting forests creates evil by destroying a landbase. Good and evil, a dichotomy different from night and day — night and day may change slightly depending on longitude but do not exist as a cultural meme that can morph within a people. Night and day exist outside our control, as do hot and cold (to the extent that we cannot alter them indefinitely). But we can control our perception of good and evil quite easily, and that makes for a very dangerous cultural meme.

It should not surprise anyone that the notion of *good* in civilization generally equates to an action based on an individual's ability to do extra work. "Do a good turn daily," says the Boy Scout motto. "Do unto others..." Helping an old lady across the street, volunteering for a cause, giving away your hard-earned money: all involve going out of your way. It makes perfect sense, then, that the noble savage myth came about. Civilized people could not understand how indigenous peoples experienced such ease with activities like sharing. *They must have better qualities than us*, reasoned our civilized ancestors.

The best example of this I find in modern culture involves the nonprofit sector of environmental education, a mass of organizations struggling to make ends meet in order to teach children about nature. Most employees work forty- to eighty-hour weeks and receive very little money for this work. It makes me cry just thinking about it. These people feel the destruction so deeply that they sacrifice themselves to keep alive a spark of love for the landbase. To people living close to the land, the idea of a nature camp would seem ludicrous. Teaching children about ecology simply works as part of their culture, not as an extra element that parents pay for. And what do these camps do but keep a spark alive? They don't change civilization; they merely work to keep children inspired to do something. What that something involves, who knows? I haven't seen any results even remotely close to what the planet needs to survive at this point.

Rewilding usurps the notion of good and evil, right and wrong, by eliminating the cultural variable and thinking in terms of environmental systems, of the physical world. If you do damage to the environment, you will experience the consequences. *Right* and *wrong*, *good* and *evil* have little bearing on that.

Indigenous cultures do not separate their religion from the land they live on. This means their religion comes from their relationship to the land, not from the "spirit," unless they mean the same thing. At Art of Mentoring gatherings, Jon Young tells how one of his Lakota mentors explained that the word people have commonly translated as *sacred* actually means "inspired by or promoting life." What our English translators have taken to mean "holy" or "revered for its spiritual significance" actually means something much more. It seems a lot less "wu-wu" when the word has real world application and not just some mystical quality. A "sacred" ceremony or ritual creates more life, and not just human life but other-than-human life as well. As my good friend Willem puts it, "*Sacred* means survival."

An interesting perspective on the Mayans comes from Martín Prechtel, who lived with Mayans (500 years post-collapse) for fifteen years. He speaks of the Mayan spiritual concept of original debt:

> In the Mayan worldview, we are all born owing a spiritual debt to the other world for having created us, for having sung us into existence. It must be fed; otherwise, it's going to take its payment out of our lives...You have to give a gift to that which gives you life. It's an actual payment in kind. That's the spiritual economy of a village.
>
> A knife, for instance, is a very minimal, almost primitive tool to people in a modern industrial society...But for the Mayan people, the spiritual debt that must be paid for the creation of such a tool is great...So, just to get the iron, the shaman has to pay for the ore, the fire, the wind, and so on—not in dollars and cents, but in ritual activity equal to what's been given...All of those ritual gifts make the knife enormously "expensive," and make the process quite involved and time-consuming. The need for ritual makes some things too spiritually expensive to bother with...That's why the Mayans didn't invent space shuttles or shopping malls or backhoes.

Civilization would feel too spiritually expensive in this paradigm, a paradigm that came about after the culture collapsed and yet that reflects many of the spiritual beliefs of never-approaching-civilization cultures that practiced intensification of food production. The more anthropologists discover about indigenous intensification of food production, the more they come to the conclusion that it does not reflect a one-way path to agriculture and civilization, but that indigenous peoples can exist in larger densities without exploiting the land and becoming agriculturalists. Values and ethics largely shape a culture's decision-making and practices.

Rewilding our ethics looks like working to make the web of life tighter. Rather than promoting ungrounded, changeable ideas of good and evil, it stems from cause and reaction in the real world: if you do damage to the environment, you do damage to your culture; if you strengthen the environment, you strengthen your culture. Let's get rid of the right and wrong, good and evil dichotomy and ask ourselves: Will it kill us? Does it meet the needs of the environment? Will it meet the needs of future generations? We need a healthy physical world to continue living. Indigenous ethics base themselves on the needs of the physical world, whereas civilization has become so far removed it doesn't even recognize a physical world. Rewilding buries right and wrong back in the land where they belong.

Religion vs. Rewilding

Do hunter-gatherers have religion? That question makes about as much sense as asking if hunter-gatherers have language, science, or art. Of course they do. But their religions look vastly different from the religions (and science and art) we find in civilization.

Like any cultural descriptor, the word *religion* evokes all kinds of emotions and images. When I think of religion I see a cross, cathedrals, a man with a long white beard sitting on a throne in the clouds, looking down with a scrutinizing eye. I remember going to church as a child and never really understanding just what the fuck people did there. I hated singing the songs in church because I couldn't read them out of the hymnal because I couldn't read. So I would rock back and forth in the pews and move around like a lion in a cage until my mom would ask me to sit still. The words the preacher said made no sense and sounded totally boring. Not to mention the stink of the mold in the old churches. Eventually I would get a headache and begin to hate my life. I never believed in god.

As with everything civilization creates, the more recent the creation, the more destructive. Science, the latest, greatest religion, follows this thread. Science claims to distinguish itself from religion by basing itself on observation of the natural world rather than mythology. I loved science. In school I always did well in science. I didn't learn until later that the institution of science also bases itself in the same mythological roots as any other civilized religion. Sciences that actually project a more accurate perception of reality (the ones that articulate a living world) get put in a box called "quantum physics" or "pseudoscience" and find themselves placed high on a shelf where we can forget about them.

Funding for science (which really means investing in building more machines that can measure things we don't trust our own senses to measure, on account of their inherent subjectivity) only goes to projects that further the civilizational paradigm. Though science masquerades as "objective inquiry," you can only fund scientific projects that somehow further the progression of civilization, and therefore the extraction of more "resources" and more interesting ways of killing people. *Science* refers to the funded exploration of the world through the belief that the world has no life, that everything exists for our exploitation.

A few sciences, like quantum physics, reveal some of the gaps in previous scientific thought. We can use these gaps to change the minds of those who believe the mythology of science. Similarly, I'll bet we could find verses in the Bible to support rewilding and the dismantling of civilization, as opposed to using the Bible to justify devouring the earth, as mainstream Christians do. (After all, the very first chapter describes humans as superior to other animals and the earth—a myth mainstream scientists use, too, to torture monkeys and build atom bombs.) Trying to rewild the institution of organized religion proves just as difficult as trying to rewild the institution of science, since both came about through civilization. We cannot rewild civilization since it never had wildness to begin with. We use the words *religion* and *science* to describe phenomena that civilization has twisted for its own purposes. We *can* rewild these things.

In order to rewild religion we have to see what myths civilization uses to domesticate it members. Salvation and sky-based god(s) only exist in civilized cultures, or in cultures already assimilated into civilization. Civilized religions demand that we struggle in this life so that god will reward us with eternal bliss in the afterlife. I can't think of a better way of stopping a slave class from revolting. (Um...aside from convincing people that a slave class no longer exists.)

Animism refers to the religions of indigenous peoples around the world. In a general sense it refers to all religions which believe that everything (even inanimate objects) has a spirit. Using a blanket term to describe thousands of religions sounds rather obnoxious to me, though it does say something about the evolutionary value of religion. It would make sense that in order to survive in the long run, people must treat everything in the world as sacred. What more sacred way of living in the world than "seeing" spirit in everything? If you don't value life, or what we commonly refer to as "inanimate" objects, you will generally consume rather than respect it.

From an animist perspective, gods live among us, not above us. They live as our parents, not hierarchical rulers. They make up an extension of our family. Some gods live as parents (Father Sun), others as siblings (Sister Corn). Living in this world, in this time, experiencing this place, not disassociating from it or anticipating an afterlife.

The literalism with which modern civilized people experience mythology astounds me. Most Christians actually believe that Adam and Eve lived as real people. In the same way, scientists can worship "facts" (or even perceive theories as laws). This probably stems from speaking English for a thousand years, a language with no built-in metaphor, layering of archetypes, or fluidity.

I generally refer to these two perceptions as *animist religions* and *civilized religions*. But *civilized religions* does little to explain just how religion and science share the same mythology. We need a blanket term for religions that see things as inanimate. A word like *inanimism*. If *animism* refers to the belief that all things have a spirit, *inanimism* refers to the belief that only humans have a spirit.

Many people conflate the institution of science with the inquiry called *science*. I generally use the term *tracking* (linking tracks and sign) to refer to an animist form of inquiry. I hardly think of animism as a religion in the institutional way we typically think of religions. I define it more as a way of perceiving the world: "spiritual, not religious." Tracking connects you to spirit, whereas civilized science dissociates people from spirit and offers the world of "meatspace." The civilized have an easier time devouring the world when they can convince themselves it never had its own life. This shows us why a subjective science (one that does not see *inanimate objects* but *living spirits*) came about through millions of years of human evolution.

I have heard many people refer to the physical world as "meatspace," as though you can split reality into two parts, a physical one and a spiritual one. I can only see one point in doing this, and that involves objectifying something in the physical world. If I can take the spirit out of something, it doesn't feel as bad when I objectify it. I feel highly offended when I hear the term "meatspace." I never really put my finger on it until my friend Willem said that it reminded him of the objectifying slang term "meat curtains" (referring to a woman's vagina).

Meat, a piece of flesh that no longer resembles the animal it came from, quite literally has no more spirit, because the animal that it came from no longer lives. From an animist's perspective, flesh and spirit do not exist as a duality but as one. Meat still holds the spirit of the animal and becomes part of your spirit when you eat it, just as the flesh becomes part of your flesh.

People for the Ethical Treatment of Animals (PETA) has offered a one-million-dollar reward for the first scientist who can clone meat. Apparently meat grown in a petri dish has no nerve endings and no way to scream (and obviously in PETA's eyes no soul), and therefore growing meat in a petri dish and eating meat from a petri dish does not violate animal ethics. Though the petri-meat may carry the label "cruelty free," the worldview and culture that would even consider inventing such a thing cannot and will not stop abusing the planet. The complete disconnection from reality, the complete disconnection from taking responsibility for and honoring the beings who die so that we may live, looks completely and utterly insane. I wish I could offer a one-million-dollar reward for the first person to bring me *the head* of the first scientist who clones meat.

How long before some perverted scientist clones a vagina in order to have sex with it? Does it count as rape if the vagina has no connection to a brain or mouth and cannot scream? If we say that cloned meat has no life, do we define having sex with a cloned vagina as necrophilia? Does a cloned vagina count as dead, or something else? This example shows exactly the kind of psychotic disassociation from reality that feeds science and projects the duality of flesh and spirit. You don't learn to live in the world through objectifying it; you learn by subjecting yourself to its terms.

Furthermore, I don't define science as "objective inquiry" because *no such thing exists*. If you remove variables, you get false information: beings do not have isolated essences but define themselves through their environment and interactions. Even if people could remove their own perceptions (which frame all inquiries and make them subjective) we would still receive false information because our perceptions define how we interact with the environment, which defines us. Even if we built a robot with no heart, it would still give us false information because the framing of its heartlessness still has subjectivity of *heartlessness*. Entities without hearts (or people who shield their own so that they feel nothing when building nukes or torturing lab rats) subjectively perceive the world in a false light, or at least in a light that does not serve life. Objectivity involves seeing things as inanimate, apart from what gives them life.

If we remove our senses, experiences, and perceptions as humans *shaped by the environment*, we remove the very things that *make us human*. We amputate our humanity, rendering useless all information pertaining to the experience of living as humans. When we no longer trust our own bodies, senses, and experiences as a measure for what we perceive as "real," we have nothing "real" at all.

For some people (myself included), rewilding religion may look like walking away from any and all inanimist religions and starting over with animism. Since I have never participated in a culture of civilized religion or science, I find it easier to build something new than fix something old and falling apart that I don't understand. For those who *do* have deep cultural ties to civilized, inanimist religions, rewilding those religions will look like rewilding the English language: it will happen very slowly over time...and those who don't change their perception will die. Animism shows us religions that stand the test of evolution. Civilization's religions will die along with civilization unless they fundamentally change through re-animating. You will need to act as a "re-animator" (just like the movie!).

Religions (whether science, Christianity, Judaism, Hinduism, Buddhism, Scientology, inanimism, or animism) dictate our choices as a culture. These religions give us justification for the way we interact with the world. Civilization uses the perception of the world as a dead thing to justify its destruction. Animism sees the world as alive and treats it accordingly. Whether or not you personally believe in spirits, in order to create a new way of life that does not destroy the planet, we need to at least pretend, with sincerity, as though everything has a spirit.

Cities vs. Rewilding

I can't help but feel like many people still hold purist values when it comes time to understand rewilding. I often hear people say, "If you want to rewild, shouldn't you go live out in the wilderness?" Rewilding means undoing domestication. Cities mark the most domesticated places in the world. Rewilding in the city has no contradictory values; it just means more work in some ways, less in others.

Cities represent the apex of civilization; they give civilization its name. Everything in the city comes from the country and wilderness. Most pollution and disease exists in these densely populated areas. Undomesticating yourself in a city looks at times like taking a walk on the interstate: defying the break-neck speed and momentum of the culture. Thinking in terms of collapse, cities will not open up for rewilding quickly, and may mark the last places we will undomesticate.

The notion of *wilderness* as an untouched place does not accurately represent reality. I still see a large division between what we commonly call wilderness (a more wild place) and urban space (a nearly completely domesticated place). But we must acknowledge that civilization has tainted every place on this earth, some places much more than others. "Wild" places have a larger opportunity for rewilding because they sit the farthest from the centers of civilization.

Waging a war against civilization while living in a city doesn't look like the smartest strategy for those who wish to survive collapse. Trouble lies around every corner, whether you call trouble a mugger, a rapist, a cop, a car, a drunk, your boss, or toxic air. I don't mean to say that those dangers don't exist in the country, just that they exist *less*. Civilization × 10 = cities. Country = civilization ÷ 10. Less-civilized people, less-civilized problems. We've all heard the statistics that your chances of attack while wandering alone in the wilderness have no comparison to wandering alone in the city. Predators don't go to the middle of nowhere to find prey, they go to where they will have an easy time catching them: densely populated areas.

A city's greatest weakness—population density, which requires the importation of resources—can also work as its greatest strength to those who rewild. Cities work as large social networks. Most people in cities have much more open "education" than those in rural areas. Large-scale cultural change happens in cities and filters out. This contrasts with the country, where neighbors who used to get the news from word of mouth now get it from Fox News via satellite TV. This may change as more people and media find their way onto the Internet, but having a solar-powered satellite Internet hook-up out in the boonies doesn't look sustainable either. Face-to-face social networking and information exchange may prove the most valuable resource a city can provide to those who rewild.

If we see the city as a resource for social networking, we can use it to our advantage, leveraging social connections to build rewilding cultures outside the city. For example, we can use the larger market of Portland to promote Rewild Camps in order to reach more people, then hold classes where the wild things live and eventually buy land out there. In a funny way, rewilding functions the opposite way a city does: it exports people and social "resources" out of the city and into the wild.

In the city we consume the resources brought from the country. In the country we watch the extraction of resources, the devouring of life: countless clear-cuts, imprisoned and tortured animals, poisoned crops burning through the soil. This feels to me like the worst part of living in the country. In the city, you can buy meat without noticing how the animal suffered, and the wood used to build your house doesn't look like a logging truck carrying the corpses of freshly murdered forests. You can't have the satisfaction of disassociation in the country. This makes it harder psychologically (in some ways) to live in the country, though at least you can see where the "resources" come from and bear witness to the destruction. When I spend time living in the country, I see exactly what the city does to the land. And what the city offers up as a resource—diversity of people and perspectives—the country lacks. Fox News plays on every bar television screen. I see "Jesus Saves" and "American Pride" bumper stickers everywhere I turn. But in the end, at this point, the pros outweigh the cons.

My early times in Molalla

Over the past month and a half I have experienced city withdrawal. I have experienced nostalgia for the years I spent drinking and sleeping around and experiencing the "night life" of the city, even though I hated those years while I lived them. I have felt completely uncomfortable and felt "bearingless," without a 3D neurological map corresponding to the physical places in my life. I have felt afraid of not looking "right" (or "too gay") to prejudiced country folk and getting beat up. I have argued with Penny Scout over our decision to move out here. The painful withdrawal reached its climax last week when I found out that most fruit you buy at the store comes from the same "mother tree" that we have cloned over and over again for hundreds of years through a perverse method called grafting. The same shocking feeling came to me that I experienced at five when I found out my burger came from a cow.

Four key elements have allowed me to make it through city withdrawal: 1) My family lives here now. 2) I have a girlfriend who lives and rewilds with me. 3) I have a large yard to learn gardening and permaculture. 4) I have a job at an awesome company that does its best to promote food self-sufficiency (in civilized terms).

My addiction finally broke this week when my buddy Billy came out and we tromped through the foothills of the Cascades. We didn't do anything special other than express our natural curiosity for living wild, and had a grand adventure I will never forget. We tracked bobcat, raccoon, and aplodontia, foraged fresh greens, met never-before-seen plants and secret waterfalls, all without any more effort than simply rolling out of bed and taking a walk. Out here in the woods I don't need to make up an adventure: adventure finds me. In ten minutes I can drive to one of the largest wild places in Oregon. I can ride my bike there in forty-five minutes. In thirty minutes I can drive where no one will ever find me. I can ride my bike there in a few hours. In the country I can spend tons of time alone, learning plants, breathing fresh air, and avoiding cops, robbers, and hippies. This week I finally feel comfortable, at home in Molalla. Now that I have settled in here, I do not feel alone. I do not crave the city nor its neon-bright addictive culture. I have a foothold and can start importing my friends from the city. Who will come with me? Show me the money!

"Green" vs. Rewilding

I recently saw a comic (thanks, Anthropik!) that inspired me to articulate some things about the notion of *greenwashing*, and other terms floating around in Mother Culture's myth-space or meme-pool. The cartoon showed a logger using an electric chainsaw.

At the illustrator's site, this comment ran alongside his drawing:

> This cartoon idea sprang fully formed from a *New York Times* piece on the ridiculous lengths that some brands are going to be considered for the Home Depot Eco Options promotion (including, yes, a brand of electric chainsaw). It's a good example of some of the outlandish greenwashing we're all starting to see. And, how the issue is not as white and black as the old treehugger/lumberjack dynamic.

I thought about this for several minutes and posted this response:

> This cartoon feels very funny and also very sad...To think that destroying more habitat (aka biodiversity) and the very life forms that filter the carbon out of the air appears "okay" simply because the technology we use to do it...functions differently. It still took an oil economy and oil energy to build the chainsaw, and it still damages

the environment by cutting down the trees and destroying more habitat for civilization's expansion.
It still looks just as cut and dry to me, only it may
feel harder to see that with all the mythology out
there.

I didn't feel satisfied with this response, though. I thought
about not just the concept of greenwashing but the actual
meaning of the term *green* in this context. We hear "green
this" and "eco that" or "environmentally friendly" and
"sustainable" and treat them as synonyms.

If the true meaning of sustainability involves giving back
more than you take from the land, then nothing that takes
more from the land than it returns can define itself as
sustainable. "Less destructive" does not mean "more sustainable." I think "more sustainable" would mean giving
even more back and not simply taking less.

If *green* does not include the real definition of sustainability but just means "less destructive," then it must mean
the same thing as *greenwashing*. In order to use the
phrase "more sustainable" you have to have sustainability
to begin with. To say that hybrid cars have more sustainability than Hummers makes no sense. They cause less
destruction (in theory). You want to know the real meaning of "environmentally friendly," "green," and "eco?" It
means that civilization leaves its rape victim alive when
it finishes taking what it wants, rather than outright mur-
dering her.

As I stood pissing in the bathroom of a movie theater, I
read a small plaque above the urinal that said something
like, "This urinal does not use water; you just helped
conserve 40,000 gallons of water a year." I couldn't help
but think, "You mean I just allocated 40,000 more gallons
of water for corporations to use at their will." We live in a

culture and economy of constant growth. *Conservation* either means saving for later consumption, as with national forests, or redistributing to other (most likely industrial) consumers. I mentioned this also in my chapter about how the vegan diet actually does more damage, as it allocates more land for grains, which produce more people than cattle, adding to the overall population growth problem and therefore more deforestation. Conservation does not amount to cultural vision change. As long as civilization continues to grow, conservation does not really exist. That doesn't mean we shouldn't try to conserve what we have left of the environment, but we must also see through the bullshit mythology. Conservation does nothing if civilization continues to grow and exploit every last "resource" it can as it collapses.

I find myself becoming angry at these words and concepts, as civilization appropriates our words and ideals before we even have the chance to articulate them. "Finally people will know the truth about global warming. Finally they will know we must abandon ship...Wait, what did you say? Um...Buy light bulbs?" I mean, sure, buy less destructive stuff, but know that it continues to destroy us.

To frame our unsustainable civilization in terms of its "sustainability" creates false hope for those just discovering the problems we face, or acts as a form of denial for those who simply can't imagine a world without civilization. Eco chainsaws do not exist. Green energy does not exist. *Get it through your fucking heads.* We've reached the end of the line.

Engineered Crisis vs. Rewilding

I keep hearing people say we've got an energy crisis. This carries a few bullshit premises. The most obvious premise here: that we need "energy." Why do we need energy? What does it do that's so fucking important? Humans lived for millions of years without electricity. Indigenous hunter-gatherers had no need to create it. It requires an entire industrial economy that inherently destroys the land in order to create it. It does not make humans' lives easier; it simply gives the rich more power and more destructive tools. How many people in the world even have electricity? We don't need energy. At least not in the way they mean it. The energy crisis, as well as the economic crisis, really means that rich people continue to lose power, and they have so brainwashed us that we believe we need to do our part to keep the pyramid strong, maintain our slavery. Civilization uses energy to take even more than we could without it. The less energy civilization has, the more limits it has to grow. That seems pretty fucking fantastic to me.

Nature provides all the energy we need in a sustainable way, as proven by three million years of human hunter-gatherers living on this planet without fucking it up. Think about the energy hunter-gatherers use: seal blubber candle vs. light bulbs, wood cooking fire vs. gas stove. Not only do hunter-gatherers have smaller-scale societies (because they don't have agriculture-induced population growth problems) but their energy usage comes from "renewable" sources. They use the sun to dry food and wood to generate heat in the cold. This burning helps to break down the nutrients and minerals in the wood and make them readily available to fungi and bacteria. It also prevents the insanely destructive, large-scale forest fires we see so often today.

Without cheap oil or coal to generate electricity and machinery, the industrial economy cannot exist. They call it "industrial" because machines (slaves, drones, robots) make it up, not people. Before industrial machinery, those in power used people. But it takes a slave with a stick a lot more time and energy to till a field than a farmer on his tractor. This excess of energy created the urban class of people, to manage the wealth (for the wealthy) created by these new machines. Real renewable energy does not mean a solar-powered industrial economy. It means small-scale societies using handmade tools (crafted from nonindustrial materials) to encourage more biodiversity.

I don't mean to say that everyone "should" stop using electricity and gas and everything—as long as you recognize you won't have it forever, and as long as you use that excess energy to bring down civilization and promote cultures of rewilding. I use a computer, cell phone, car, and all sorts of technology to educate people on how to live without them, and encourage people to stop these systems from destroying the planet. Remember, *green* technology doesn't mean "more sustainable" but "less destructive." And more often it really means "We've reframed our marketing to pull the focus away from what we destroy, to point out what we don't destroy, so that you'll forget that we continue to fuck shit up."

People have barked up my tree over this whole economic

crisis as well. You know what? I don't give a shit! We've seen economic collapses before. In fact they work as a normal function of civilization; and like clockwork, they merely end with the creation of a worse slave system than before. One world currency, one world culture. America has amassed a lot of fake wealth, weapons, and technology. But why go to the third world for labor when you can bring the third world to you? I don't see economic collapse as the end of civilization but as a reorganization of wealth that will end with a stronger pyramid: more people on the bottom and fewer people on top. Like the climate and energy crises, the economic collapse has not triggered anyone to actually stop civilization, walk away, or rewild. It appears that it will simply mean more people working longer hours for less money in shittier jobs than before.

I refer to these crises that we really have going on as the "bullshit crisis." Everyone listens to this civilized bullshit and takes it in without question, and the world continues to suffer. That looks like the real fucking crisis to me. The *ecological crisis*. This crisis only exists because we *have* an "economy" and "energy." The economic crisis means the end of growth, which means the end of excessive consumption, which means the beginning of the end of the ecological crisis. Fuck industrial energy, fuck the hierarchical economy, fuck this bullshit.

Guilt vs. Rewilding

Guilt refers to the feeling we have when we make decisions that go against personal, cultural, and mythological pressures. It feels like not doing what you "should" do. It works as one of the most powerful tools of social and cultural maintenance. I do not think of guilt as a "bad" thing. I see it as a tool we need to understand. Rewilding goes against all of our lifelong civilized programming. Anything we do to rewild could make us feel guilty. Of course, the culture of rewilding creates a new paradigm in which continuing to live in civilization would make us feel guilty since we know that civilization destroys biodiversity. In a sense, rewilding involves crossing a threshold into two worlds. This creates a split cultural psyche, leaving us with weird schizophrenic emotions: feeling guilty for leaving civilization as well as for not having left enough. For example, one might experience guilt for not going to college and simultaneously for using gasoline.

It works like this. We learn that civilization destroys the planet, our senses, and a million other things. We learn that indigenous peoples had their needs met without destroying the planet. This gets most people thinking that all humans should abandon the nonworking model of civilization and live sustainably like the indigenous peoples we read about—that we have to, or we will die! Though urgent and emotionally true, to think that we can merely abandon civilization and build a sustainable culture with this awareness ignores the context in which these cultures formed: via the *needs* of a hunter-gatherer culture. The culture of civilization, in which we all live as captives, makes it extremely difficult to exist with even a shred of freedom.

In rewilding, these indigenous cultures represent human potential. They remind us that life doesn't have to feel like slavery. And yet we can't just throw on buckskin clothes, make a bow and arrow, and live as they did. Without a physical, cultural, social, and emotional need for creating a rewilding culture, it exists only as something we can try to live up to. Our cultural momentum carries us towards domestication. Why learn to hunt and gather when you can just get a job and buy food at the store? You don't need to know much more than how to use a cash register and how to microwave your Cup-a-Soup to get by. Yet we know we must defy civilization and its economy of death if we wish to save the world. This leaves us with one foot shackled to civilization as the other foot gains footing in the wild.

Rewilding creates two opposing systems of perception in our heads and hearts. One says we need to buy flat-screen TVs to see the quality of HDTV; the other says we need to sit in a forest for an hour each day to connect more with nature. One of these systems kills the planet. We can't simply reprogram our brains. Every day the brain rewires itself. Every cultural element tells us what to think (or continue thinking), from our newspaper to our TV shows, to whatever we hear while eavesdropping on the bus, and even to the buildings that surround us. Our minds reflect our environment, and vice versa. We can't just read a book on rewilding and change how we see the world. We need to change *everything* about our world.

Guilt only works to make the journey from civilized to

wild harder. My strongest experience with this guilt came from trying to replicate an indigenous cultural ritual known as the sit spot. I had trouble making this routine for two main reasons. First, sitting in the woods may have given hunter-gatherers skills and awareness essential to their survival, but it does not relate to subsistence within a civilizational context. Your secret spot does not give you an edge if you work in a coffee shop. Generally speaking, having a sit spot will not make you more money, the way it would yield better food results for hunter-gatherers.

As civilization destroys more and more of the wild environment, we have seen our internal environments, those of the mind and heart, suffer as well. Some people may have trouble functioning psychologically and need a more natural setting to calm their minds. Unfortunately, seeking the wilderness seems to appear as taboo, and the vast majority of people (behaving the way the culture of civilization designed us to behave) choose an easier way to alleviate their minds with the use of drugs, TV, video games, and everything else.

It takes will power to go against the grain and choose the harder path to sanity, especially when sanity doesn't show up on the list of requirements to live and work in civilization. In fact, I would say that insanity seems like a requirement for those who continue to destroy the land from which they live. Therefore indigenous practices like the sit spot become a ritual for the pure, which can feel more difficult to choose than the available alternatives. If having a sit spot gives you more empathy towards the earth, which it did for me, it may in fact have the reverse effect of subsistence within civilization, where you have to shut off connection to nature in order to function in the city. In short, it may make you hate your job, hate your current life, and in turn lead to you making less money.

Because rewilding works against subsistence in a civilizational context, and takes more effort than simply taking
drugs (Prozac, cigarettes, television, video games, etc.), it
will always fall into the category of self-help. This means
that during any kind of increase in level of stress, routines
unnecessary to subsistence will get placed on the back
burner. For example, if you need to work more hours at
your job, that means less time rewilding. This shows how
trapped we become in civilization. This feeling of entrap-
ment feels even worse once compounded with guilt.

The guilt one feels at "choosing the easy way out" appears the worst part of the self-help category. Although
choosing the easy way out or the path of least resistance
feels like a normal human response, we feel a kind of
failure when we make this "choice." Because we want
awareness and the gifts that come with it, because of the
mythology that surrounds this awareness and lifestyle
(that it represents our birth right, that it reveals how the
gods meant us to live, and so forth), when we follow our
instincts that say "Follow the path of least resistance," we
feel a kind of guilt similar to what I imagine Christians
must feel when they commit a sin.

This guilt made me hate the sit spot routine and rewilding
in general. For several years the books, journals, and field
guides filling up a large bookshelf in the center of my
room collected dust. I wanted the awareness and knowledge, but I, like most people, had no cultural context for
rewilding. I blamed myself for following what civilization
programmed me to do. Every time I looked at the books
I felt guilty. I had built a shrine of guilt in the center of
my own room. "Why don't I like rewilding anymore?" I
would ask myself.

One day during a moment of clarity and transition in my
life, I burned my sit spot journals and sold my entire field

guide library to a local bookstore. It felt like taking a huge dump after being constipated for years; I felt a release and a great weight lifted. When I arrived home on that clear winter evening, the sun had just begun to set and the sky looked a beautiful reddish-purple hue. I felt so light and happy that I actually wanted to go to my sit spot: the burden of becoming a super-indigenous, hyper-aware human had gone. When I finished I looked again to the sky. At that moment a red-tailed hawk gracefully and quietly snatched a pigeon out of the air, not five feet above my head. The hawk landed in my neighbor's yard and began to tear the pigeon to pieces. I watched in total awe. I think of it as nature's gift to a guilt-free heart.

I have always loved this quote by Joseph Campbell:

> If you follow your bliss, you put yourself on a kind of track that has been there all the while, waiting for you, and the life that you ought to be living is the one you are living. Wherever you are—if you are following your bliss, you are enjoying that refreshment, that life within you, all the time.

What makes suffering different from torture? Even when suffering you still have that refreshment Campbell speaks of to keep you going. In fact, sometimes that feeling of passion feels strongest during more difficult moments. But if you have no passion, suffering becomes torture. Torture looks like suffering for the sake of suffering, without any of the "refreshment" Campbell speaks of. I remember another quote in the same vein from Martín Prechtel:

> There are two kinds of suffering, one that creates beauty and one that creates more suffering.

Guilt, in the context of rewilding, only creates more suffering by distracting people from the important things.
Who cares if I watch *Battlestar Galactica* instead of gathering wapato? Obviously I don't do that every day, but
everyone needs a break (or two or three) from "saving
the world." I do not believe in purity and therefore feel
no guilt from indulging in civilization every once in a
while. (I would like to add, though, that addiction works
differently from indulgence and needs a different kind of
attention.)

I still experience this schizophrenic guilt every day. Right
now, even as I type this, I feel guilty for not going outside.
As long as we feel guilty for not having the tools or culture
to break the shackles that chain us here, we strengthen
civilization's hold on us.

Science vs. Rewilding

I remember feeling ill at the thought of libraries (full of books containing knowledge gained through science) burning down during the collapse of civilization. All that knowledge—lost forever. I used to believe that, despite all the terrible things civilization has created. Science felt worth saving. For some reason I saw science as something "pure" that even civilization's mythology could not ruin. I don't feel that way anymore. These days a wry smile forms on my face, and my eyes begin to sparkle when I envision a world without science.

Did science exist before civilization? Well, that depends on your definition of science. According to the *American Heritage Science Dictionary*, the word *science* means:

> The investigation of natural phenomena through observation, theoretical explanation, and experimentation, or the knowledge produced by such investigation. Science makes use of the scientific method, which includes the careful observation of natural phenomena, the formulation of a hypothesis, the conducting of one or more experiments to test the hypothesis, and the drawing of a conclusion that confirms or modifies the hypothesis

We know now that the modern human has not evolved substantially in at least 100,000 years. Our modern brains have no significant difference from our hunter-gatherer ancestors. But our lineage of hunting goes much further than that. Evolution occurs mostly through the methods animals use to acquire food, water, and shelter: natural selection. Hunting and gathering has long had an impact on hominid evolution. Since animal tracking forms the critical aspect of hunting, the ability to track animals most likely shaped the modern mind.

According to Louis Liebenberg, author of *The Art of Tracking: The Origin of Science*,

> Speculative tracking involves the creation of a working hypothesis on the basis of initial interpretation of signs, a knowledge of animal behavior and a knowledge of the terrain. Having built a hypothetical reconstruction of the animal's activities in their mind, the trackers then look for signs where they expect to find them.

> In contrast to simple and systematic tracking (following clear prints, such as in sand or snow), speculative tracking is based on hypothetico-deductive reasoning, and involves a fundamentally new way of thinking.

Liebenberg's description of tracking falls quite nicely into the definition of science we see above. The term *tracking* generally refers to following animal tracks. But to most indigenous peoples I have studied, the concept of tracking includes much more than following animal prints. According to Tom Brown Jr., the Apache did not differentiate between *tracking* and *awareness*. Martín Prechtel has said that in his indigenous Guatemalan village they referred to their shamans as *trackers*. In the film *The Great Dance: A Hunter's Story*, we learn that the Kalahari Bushmen's word for tracking means the same thing as dancing.

More Liebenberg:

I would argue that the differences between the art of tracking and modern science are mainly technological and sociological. Fundamentally they involve the same reasoning processes and require the same intellectual abilities. The modern scientist may know much more than the tracker, but he/she does not necessarily understand nature any better than the intelligent hunter-gatherer. What the expert tracker lacks in quantity of knowledge (compared to modern scientists), he/she may well make up for in subtlety and refinement. The intelligent hunter-gatherer may be just as rational in his/her understanding of nature as the intelligent modern scientist. Conversely, the intelligent modern scientist may be just as irrational as the intelligent hunter-gatherer. One of the paradoxes of progress is that, contrary to expectation, the growth of our knowledge about nature has not made it easier to reach rational decisions.

Despite "progress" in science and technology, the people of civilization have never slowed their destruction of the planet. That strikes me as a very strange paradox indeed. For such a great culture of rationalists, it seems extremely irrational to destroy the land on which we all depend for survival. Why have hunter-gatherers thrived for hundreds of thousands of years, while civilization has decimated the entire planet after only ten thousand? It seems the "technological and sociological" differences might have a much more fundamental weight than Liebenberg presumes.

By looking at the sociological differences between agricultural subsistence versus hunter-gatherer subsistence we see just how different science and tracking really manifest.

Hunting and gathering by its nature demands participation in the ebb and flow of life. You have no more control over your food supply than any other animal. That doesn't mean that you do not encourage the biodiversity of your area, it just means that you don't spend all your time tilling a monocropped field. Sometimes the gods grace you with food, other times not. But rarely do you go hungry. Hunter-gatherers do not have to work at having a deep relationship with nature; the relationship simply shapes how they behave. Tracking shapes their reality, deepening their connection to the land with every track they read.

> The first track is the end of a string. At the far end, a being is moving; a mystery, dropping a hint about itself every so many feet, telling you more about itself until you can almost see it, even before you come to it. The mystery reveals itself slowly, track by track, giving its genealogy early to coax you in. Further on, it will tell you the intimate details of its life and work, until you know the maker of the track like a lifelong friend.
>
> —Tom Brown Jr., *The Tracker*

> Ultimately, tracking an animal makes us sensitive to it—a bond is formed, an intimacy develops. We begin to realize that what is happening to the animals and to the planet is actually happening to us. We are all one. Tracking and reading sign help us to learn not only about the animals that walk around in the forest—what they are doing and where they are going—but also about ourselves. For me, this interconnection is survival knowledge and the true value of tracking an animal.
>
> —Paul Rezendes, *Tracking and the Art of Seeing*

When you track an animal—you must become the animal. Tracking is like dancing, because your

> body is happy—you can feel it in the dance and
> then you know that the hunting will be good.
> When you are doing these things you are talking
> with God.
>
> —!Nqate Xqamxebe, *The Great Dance: A Hunter's Story*

Tracking requires empathy for that which you track. Many anthropologists like to use the word *anthropomorphize*. They say that trackers project their own feelings onto the animals, thereby identifying with them both psychologically and emotionally. This helps the tracker speculate the animal's next move. I reject the ideology that hunter-gatherer trackers project their emotions onto animals. They open themselves to the animal's feelings, the same way one lets in the sounds of music. Different kinds of music evoke different kinds of feelings in the listener. You can't say that I have projected my feelings onto a sensory experience like hearing a sound. But rather I have ears that can perceive sounds. Sounds enter my ears and teach me things about how I feel. When you step on a dog's foot and hear it whimper and then feel bad for the dog, you have not projected feelings of pain onto the dog; you have observed a dog in obvious pain and have opened your sense of empathy for the dog's feelings. Or maybe you don't care. Maybe you cut their vocal chords in preparation for a vivisection.

Tracking requires humility, not just toward the animals you track but also toward the gods who provide you with food. Hunter-gatherers must have humility. The word *humble* comes from *humus*, which means "close to the earth." Empathy helps you to realize we all live together in the same space (plants, animals, rocks, clouds, etc.) as a big family. The realization that we all live as a family gives us humility as a small part of a large creation. You must have humility when your life rests in the hands of this natural community.

Liebenberg wrote something else I thought sounded interesting:

> Religious belief is so fundamental to the hunters' way of thinking that it cannot be separated from hunting itself. At the end of the day, if they have had no luck in tracking down an animal, !XO hunters will say that the greater god did not "give" them an animal that day. If, on the other hand, they have had a successful hunt, they will say that the greater god was good to them.

Agricultural societies (civilizations), on the other hand, attempt to exert control over food supply by growing it themselves. While every other living creature leaves their food supply in the hands of fate, or the gods, or nature, agricultural people remove themselves from fate. A separation from the community of life must happen so that farmers can turn biodiverse forests into monocrop for human consumption. This violates the fundamental law in nature that no living thing takes more than it needs to survive. In order to maintain this kind of controlling relationship to the land, agricultural people must separate themselves from it psychologically and emotionally. Willem Larsen at The College of Mythic Cartography also spoke of this in his essay *Vivisecting 'The Flesh,' and the Cult of Science*:

> Our Science has propelled an immense productivity in scientific knowledge precisely because it does not consider the universe alive; it proceeds at a meteoric pace, because it need never ask permission of a dead universe, it need never pause in its breakneck progress. Because of this, it will

> also never know certain things, and actually will perpetuate a blindness of other relationships. The Scientific process actually acts as a ceremony that further inculcates the worldview of a dead universe.

Control lies at the heart of civilization. Control over food supply means control over the earth. This culture, by its very nature, lacks humility towards the earth. You cannot show empathy towards those you dominate.

Let's play with Liebenberg's quote and flip it around on itself:

> Religious belief is so fundamental to the scientists' (civilizationists') way of thinking that it cannot be separated from science (civilization) itself.

At the end of the day, if the greater god has not "given" the civilizationists food, they will ignore the god and "take" whatever they want. I think this shows us what Liebenberg meant when he said modern scientists could behave irrationally too. This means that information gathered by scientists has lacked empathy and humility, two fundamental aspects of our evolution as tracking hunter-gatherers. It also means scientists will not use the information with empathy and humility. How could they?

Tracking connects us to oneness and humility. Science separates us from that which gives us life. Although the mechanics of tracking and science seem similar, the cultural values behind the processes (humility vs. control) create very different results.

What does this mean for those who rewild? It means that, most likely, the knowledge forcefully stolen from nature by civilization's scientists will have little use, if any, to hunter-gatherer-horticulturalists. And further, that information taken (not received) without humility and empathy will in fact have deadly results in the real world.

It also means that gaining knowledge through tracking may work as one of the most important adventures in rewilding.

Image vs. Rewilding

Most birds cannot "choose" a different plumage to attract a mate. But not all birds. The bowerbird provides a rather interesting example of a bird that has externalized its image as a way of attracting a mate. This bird builds a bower with as many shiny blue things as he can find, including manmade plastic and glass. He has such a particularity about the aesthetic of his bower that he will restore the bower to his exact specifications should it become disturbed. The female chooses whether to mate with the male based on the aesthetic of the bower. The bower serves no other purpose; they abandon it and move elsewhere to make their nest.

Other animals evolved an image that would detract predators: camouflage. Brown birds have brown feathers because they live close to the ground. Some birds, such as the red-winged blackbird, can hide their bright plumage to appear more inconspicuous. They use their image to both hide from predators and attract a mate. This shows us the purpose of image, whether externalized or embedded: to attract or deter something.

Humans wear the clothes of a subculture to attract those of like mind and turn away others. I get made fun of for looking like a hipster all the time. I care a lot about my image, and I feel no guilt or lack of purity for feeling that way. I take showers, I shave, I dress in clothes that I think look cool and match the aesthetic I see as "hip." Of course, any group of culture or subculture has their specific way of dressing that allows people to recognize which culture or subculture they belong to. Each of these subcultures has their own "hip" as well.

I've noticed many people (including myself) become wrapped up in the idea that because many indigenous cultures had sustainable subsistence strategies that means all of their customs will work for everyone. Though I've found it easy to jump to this conclusion as I rewild, I have also found it more and more limiting: just because native cultures did it, doesn't mean it will work for people who rewild.

I can hear the conversation with my mom in my head. It goes like this:

> "Peter, why do you wear that loin cloth? You just look ridiculous in it!"
>
> "Mooooom! I told you, when I wear the loin cloth call me Urban Scout! You'll embarrass me!"
>
> "Oh, oh…Sorry, honey."
>
> "I wear it because primitive peoples do, and I want to live like them."
>
> "Okay, 'Scout,' and if primitive people jumped off a bridge…? I mean what do you plan to practice next, cannibalism?!?"
>
> "Of course not!" And then, under my breath, "I mean, not *yet.*"
>
> "What did you say?"
>
> "Huh?"
>
> "That last part. Did you say something else?"
>
> "What? Oh, I just mean, yeah, totally. No, what?"
>
> "Huh? Oh, not. Nothing. I thought you said something."
>
> "Nope."

"Okay, but do you see what I mean? Just because some primitive people wore a loin cloth doesn't mean you have to, too."

But seriously, I see this everywhere. It seems many people have begun to generalize indigenous customs ("Indigenous peoples did X") to justify their own level of hip. I even found this when I recently read the Crimethinc *Hunter-Gatherer* zine. Don't get me wrong: I love Crimethinc, and I enjoyed most of the zine. But I couldn't help but feel irritated with the following text:

One Million Years of d.i.y. punk!

For over 50,000 years, our ancestors didn't shave their legs or armpits or wear deodorant. They scavenged food like modern trash-pickers do, traveled like hitchhikers riding rivers and hopping ocean currents around the world, celebrated life with folk music made by their friends, passed down culture they devised. You bet some of them had dreadlocks, some homemade tattoos and scarification, some patches proclaiming their allegiances. There used to be as many humans as there are punk rockers, now.

"See how cool we...look. See our dreads? Smell our BO? See how we 'forage' in dumpsters? Don't we just act sooo indigenous/primitive?"...Hey, Crimethinc, you forgot to say 50,000 years of DIY man/boy love! Check this out:

Gilbert Herdt (1981, 1984a, 1987, 1990) and other anthropologists have reported on a pederastic puberty ritual shared by 30 to 50 Melanesian and New Guinea cultures that may be historically related to similar practices that developed among aboriginal Australians some 10,000 years ago. The focus of intense speculation by anthropologists

> and fierce opposition from Western governments
> and missionaries, these ritualized homosexual re-
> lationships are a necessary part of the coming-of-
> age training for boys. Their basis is the belief that
> boys do not produce their own semen and must get
> it from older men by "drinking semen," i.e., playing
> the recipient role in oral-genital sex or anal sex
> before puberty and during adolescence. This is the
> opposite of the traditional Western view in which
> the recipient (insertee) of anal or oral sex is robbed
> of his manhood.

Oh my god. NAMBLA (North American Man/Boy As-
sociation) acts sooo much more indigenous than punk
rockers! Since the members of NAMBLA have drank
"man's milk" and I have not (well, I did taste my own once),
does that mean they should have a blog about rewilding
and I should shut up? That makes no fucking sense at all.
People all around the world, civilized and not, practice a
multitude of customs and dogmas.

Why does this paragraph from Crimethinc frustrate me
so much? Two reasons.

The first statement, "For over 50,000 years, our ancestors
didn't shave their legs or armpits or wear deodorant,"
implies that no indigenous cultures had beautification
rituals involving hair removal and body scenting. That
doesn't hold true at all. Many cultures, such as the
Iroquois, plucked all of their body hair using clamshells.
And we know that indigenous people scented themselves
with things like lavender, rosemary, and other herbs. I
guess Crimethinc's statement does hold true in one sense:
indigenous people didn't use the industrially produced
Mach3 razor or Teen Spirit. But the passage I quoted
makes it clear that the author wants to justify why so

many DIY punk kids smell like shit and have scraggly hair all over their bodies.

You know the kids with the hippie "natural" look? In reality it has nothing to do with looking natural, since we know that many "natural" human cultures had highly maintained beautification. It really translates to the no-maintenance look. They stink and have unkempt beards or leg hair, shaggy, nappy, hair, with raggedy clothes hanging off their bodies by a thread. They might live on the anarcho-punk end of the spectrum or the pacifist-hippie end; they may wear all black, with dirt smears on their face and have steel-toed boots (how did they pay for those?!?), or they may have patchy, colorful cords with overly large tie-dye shirts and hemp sandals.

The funniest part to me about the no-maintenance look involves how much maintenance it actually takes! Seriously, I know because I dressed that way for a time. It takes a lot of work to look like you don't care. Looking like you don't care exemplifies your own cultural hipness, and you use an inaccurate perception of indigenous people to back it up.

The second reason I feel frustrated comes from this misinformation presenting a superficial reason for rewilding. It distracts us from the important reasons we yearn for the indigenous lifestyle: meeting the needs of the environment, culture, and individual. What makes the indigenous lifestyle attractive in the most general sense does not involve particular rituals, style of dress, level of cleanliness, sexual practices, or other customs. By contaminating the mythology and taking us away from the subsistence strategies of indigenous people, to the more superficial layer of image, we find ourselves never fully getting what we need. No number of sweat lodges, dreadlocks, or homemade folk songs will give us the subsistence strategy of hunting and gathering that meets the needs of all three elements mentioned above. They may keep those strategies alive once practiced, but they don't act as the strategies themselves.

While picking trash carries the same spirit as indigenous foragers, it does not serve the same function in terms of meeting the needs of the environment: picking trash does not make the ecosystem healthier, because the mechanisms that create the trash in the first place come from the larger destructive culture. While it may feel better than working as a slave in the pyramid, it does not help the ecosystem the way a hunter-gatherer culture would.

Both of these misrepresentations of indigenous culture fuel a radder-than-thou personification of those in the anarcho-primitivist-punk scene. "We act sooo much more primitive than you do, with your clean-shaven face, pressed slacks, and pop music collection." Basically it amounts to scenester trash. It only serves to alienate other people to the true ideology of indigenous living because of its falsified, superficial layer of image.

Wearing buckskin clothes or a loin cloth doesn't make you a native. Wearing all black and dreadlocks doesn't make you more anarcho-primitivist than wearing American Apparel. Rewilding refers to an action like running or climbing, it does not have a specific image. Anyone, from any subculture, can rewild. It works as a cross-cultural activity, like reading, cooking, or talking. Therefore it may look completely different to one culture or subculture to the next. Don't get lost in image. Keep your eye on the prize: living wild and free and creating more biodiversity.

everyone under thirty playing in a rock band...and no one had ever heard of myspace or youtube.

I dropped out of high school at sixteen to rewild. I took classes and spent most of my time in the woods, the library, or at my wage-slave job. I didn't care much for the way I dressed. I wore mostly oversized military surplus wool clothes. I didn't really care much about aesthetic at that point in my life because I had no culture. For the most part I lived like a loner. I quit doing anything artistic (including filmmaking) because I didn't think that would help me learn to rewild. I lived this way until I came across Joseph Campbell. Then I really began to see a purpose in my passion for art and cultural creativity. He said:

> The function of the artist is the mythologization of the environment.

I realized that my artistic talents in filmmaking and other mediums could actually help create a cultural movement of rewilding by using art to spread the mythology of it. Lonely at nineteen, with no culture of rewilders, never having had a girlfriend before, I began to spend more time with people. I realized if I wanted to create a culture of rewilding, I would need to blend in with the other artists in town, and subversively spread animism and rewilding from within the arts scene.

Luckily I had some really cool coworker friends at Coffee People to show me the ropes. We went to the Goodwill bins and I got a new wardrobe in two hours for $5. This happened back when the bins only charged 39¢ a pound and before the overpriced "vintage" thrift stores began sending their employees there to pick out all the good stuff so that they could then up-sell it. I would dig

Hipsters vs. Rewilding

Can everyone shut the fuck up about hipsters already? I feel so fucking sick of that word. The whole subject seriously bores the shit out of me, and yet I constantly have to defend myself from people who call me that as though it suddenly makes everything I have done to further rewilding insincere or fake. I usually shrug it off, but I recently surfed to the Adbusters website only to see an entire feature article from last summer where they just talk all kinds of shit about hipsters, and now I feel I need to say something.

I got called a hipster for the first time while walking into a burrito place on Belmont Street. As I walked through the door this big biker-looking dude ushered out his four-year-old son. He said to his son with disgust, "Watch out for the hipster." I remember feeling angry at first, thinking, "I'm not a fucking hipster." But of course I fit the description. I had on a vintage Ferrari T-shirt, tight black polyester Wranglers, black Ray-Ban sunglasses, black Converse, and I had a mullet. This occurred in 2003.

While growing up I saw Portland as just another quiet, small, boring city on the West Coast, always living in the shadow of Seattle and San Francisco. Thanks to former mayor Vera Katz (who hated homeless people and loved money), art galleries and fancy restaurants now litter the city. Five years ago Portland suddenly became an up-and-coming arts town, with super affordable rent, cheap beer, through the troughs of clothes, hold up a shirt for my friend Dave to see, and he would explain whether it would work and why. It felt like taking a class on how to "see" cool. Dave loves clothes, and talking about aesthetics and his excitement and knowledge spilled over into me. With Dave's wardrobe help, I found my first girlfriend, a seamstress and clothing designer who took me a few steps further, showing me how to dress for my particular body. Her classic motto at the time: "It works if you work it." With both of their help, I became a hipster fashionista practically overnight.

I can hear you all saying, "What a poseur!" Let's talk about that for a second. In high school I remember this one time walking by the most gothic kid in our school and overhearing him saying, "Then this guy was like, 'Get outta my way, you goth!' and I was like...Oh my god! I'm not gothic!" I remember thinking, "What the fuck is that guy talking about? He is obviously gothic." I knew immediately why he said it that way; it doesn't seem cool to "try" to look gothic. To label yourself as gothic would mean you went out of your way to dress like that. For some reason that breaks the rules of cool. Probably because it shows that you care, and caring about things— showing any kind of sincerity—doesn't mean cool in our dead, heartless culture.

I recently pointed out to a green anarchist who claimed to dress however he wanted that he wore all the right green anarchist scenester clothes topped off with their iconic dreadlocks. By admitting that I choose to dress this way—as a hipster—I no longer look cool because you don't look cool if you "follow the crowd." If dressing punk or gothic or hipster or anarchist supposedly means an attempt at rebelling against the mainstream, then admitting the label of hipster implies that you follow a fashion trend, which means you admit to not having your own creative individuality. Let's get real. No one dresses like an individual. No one accidentally dresses like a gutter punk, hipster, hippie, yuppie, normal core, or whatever. Everyone *chooses* their subcultural identity. You cannot wear clothes (or not wear clothes) that will not lump you in with some kind of crowd, because every way of dress implies a subculture. Subcultures create aesthetics. Your individuality comes out of how you express yourself in that particular subculture. If you dress like a gutter punk, you'll obviously have a studded jacket, but the placement of studs or the words you write on the jacket will express your own individuality within that culture.

In the years that followed I made a lot of friends, partied my ass off, and forgot all about why I became part of that subculture. At the time of this writing (2008), Portland feels like Seattle's formerly cooler punk rock cousin who finally had to get a job. In other words, the party ended. Rent costs much more, beer costs much more, and barista jobs for starving artists have disappeared. I've seen the small town turn into a huge, strung-out city practically overnight. I've lived through, identified with, and learned a tremendous amount about the rise of hipster culture. I will risk my coolness and admit that I dress like a hipster, whatever that even means.

I find it interesting that "critiques" of hipster culture never come from the hipster community speaking for itself (of course it can't if no one admits to dressing as one!) but always from an outsider talking about something they live apart from and don't understand, because they appear too old, jealous, or more self-conscious than the hipsters they attack. I rarely hear the friends I would label as hipsters talking shit about people for the way they dress or the music they listen to. I talk more shit than anyone

I know, hipster or not! I've probably heard a dozen or more people who I don't consider hipsters say, "Look at those fucking hipsters over there. They think they're so fucking cool." You know what? I bet those hipsters didn't even notice you. Why the fuck do you care? Why do you go out of your way to point them out?

Critics claim that hipsters steal symbols and styles from previous cultures but without the authenticity or sincerity of those cultures. Firstly, every new subculture steals from an older one and changes its meaning. Old people say this every time a new subculture rises. "They're stealing from us!" Generally because the old people don't feel appreciated or acknowledged for "creating" (even though they stole it from someone else!) that particular style. Secondly, in terms of lack of authenticity or sincerity, every culture adapts and alters an old style and gives it a new meaning. People complain about hipsters' lack of sincerity and meaning, but that just reflects our "new" twist.

Urban people's lives have no point. We exist as the human waste product of agriculture. We have no integrated purpose in the context of the real, wild world. We have no relationship with our landbase except blind exploitation. We exist only to serve coffee to those in power, to enter data into spreadsheets for those in power, or to operate machinery for those in power. We simply shift wealth around so that we feel like we have some worth, even though we don't. Though we drown ourselves in culture, none of it has any meaning beyond its initial consumption. We've made our entire culture disposable. We've made our lives disposable.

Some have made claims that we hipsters, unlike previous countercultures, do not rebel against previous generations. This seems like a lazy analysis to me. Hipsters *have* rebelled against previous generations; we have rebelled against *meaning*. The people of my generation have all seen what those in power do to people with feelings and ideas. We've seen the gamut of "revolutions," and we have seen that they mean nothing in the end. Civilization continues to kill all life on this planet no matter who sits in charge. No matter how much we protest, this culture wins and the earth dies. No matter what we do, we live as slaves to it. They've programmed us with pacifism from birth. Rather than look foolish like our "revolutionary" predecessors, we just stopped caring and accepted our slavery to find happiness in novelty, irony, drugs, sex, and music. Hipsters do not look lame for acting apathetic: civilization destroyed our lives, our hearts, and our landbase.

If meaninglessness looks cool now, it will not look cool tomorrow. I want to break the shackles of this hierarchy and create a living world. I feel determined to make rewilding more than just the next counterculture.

Sarcasm vs. Rewilding

Humans have a long history of teaching social taboos through jokes, irony, sarcasm, and mockery, showing us what we do not find as acceptable behavior. Such comic geniuses as Jerry Seinfeld and Larry David know this too well, their narcissistic characters always breaking social taboos and looking like assholes. In Farley Mowat's *People of the Deer* I recall a moment in which he drew a picture of a deer smoking a pipe, and the Inuits laughed hysterically. I think this kind of ridiculousness encapsulates the humor in irony, sarcasm, and mockery. It has a kind of innocence to it; it looks silly for a deer to do human things, just as it looks silly for a human to do deer things. We laugh at the ridiculousness of the situation, whether we see a deer smoking a pipe or Larry David not bringing a gift to Ben Stiller's birthday party.

After several seasons of mimicking racist stereotypes under the guise of bringing the idiocy of racism to light, Dave Chappelle changed his mind about using this kind of humor. While shooting a sketch, he noticed a white man laugh a little too hard at a racist joke, and it made him uncomfortable. Dave could tell from the way he laughed that this white guy did not get the joke. He told *TIME* magazine that he realized the irony of his racism didn't translate, so he quit the show and went on vacation.

It seems that the line between sarcasm and sincerity has a lot to do with context. If I make a joke with my friends, from the perspective of someone living a lifestyle I find abusive, they'll laugh because they'll understand the sarcasm: I would never sincerely make those comments. But if I make the same joke to people who actually have the perspective I mock, they won't get the sarcasm. Instead they will hear the joke as reinforcement for the abusive perspective.

A few years ago I heard Janis Joplin's ironic song "Mercedes Benz" in a Mercedes Benz television commercial. Oh lord, won't you buy me an AK47; my friends all have sold out—I must make amends. I can feel Janis rolling over in her grave: an anti-consumerist song used to sell consumption. (Of course, she did drive a Porsche, so maybe not.) An adbuster used as an advertisement. Ironic, don't you think? Change or remove the context of an adbuster, and it just looks like an advertisement.

I watched Steve Colbert "roast" the President of the United States for thirty minutes nonstop. Of course I laughed. But remember, the court jester had permission to insult the king. You have to ask why? If sarcasm and mockery really threatened those in power, would they allow it? Do jokes motivate you to stop injustice? Does laughter make you want to put an end to racism? Fascism? Civilization?

Most ironic and sarcastic jokes of this ilk appear to me as a kind of psychological *gallows humor*. Gallows humor refers to ironic or sarcastic jokes made by those who face the gallows in order to keep their spirits up—people who have no more options to fight back. Gallows humor works as a last resort to hold onto dignity in the face of abuse. Our domestication causes us to see our fate as slaves to civilization as something inevitable and inescapable, just as a death row inmate will inevitably sit in the electric chair. The civilized have accepted this programmed fate and do not fight it. "We can't stop our destructive culture from killing the planet, but we don't have to let it kill our morale."

While gallows humor can have a spiritually liberating quality, it doesn't physically liberate you from the noose. It merely makes living with abuse more tolerable. The question becomes, does having a higher level of morale motivate you to fight back or cause you to remain apathetic and accept your fate?

Think back to the question, "Why did the king allow the jester to insult him?" Sure, you can laugh all you want, vote all you want, petition all you want, protest all you want (as long as you stay in the designated protest area), blog all you want, and say all you want. You can even own a gun or two or three. So long as you don't actually *do* anything that threatens those in power or the progress of civilization.

If *gallows humor* refers only to the abused, *executioner's humor* refers to ironic or sarcastic jokes made by those who run the gallows in order to distance themselves from the guilt of murder. Executioner's humor says, "We refuse to change our cycle of abuse, and we will make jokes to distance ourselves from the guilt we feel when we abuse you." I can make fun of how much gas my SUV consumes because it distances me from feeling bad about it, and I don't have to change my life. I can joke about slavery in a foreign country because it makes me feel better about buying clothes from the Gap. I can make a joke about staying inside on a sunny day to watch TV because it will make me feel less guilty.

If no press equals bad press, then even making fun of abusive behaviors promotes them regardless of context, whether gallows or executioner's humor. By joking about atrocities, we promote them. By having a serious discussion about them, we allow them to continue. Perhaps we just shouldn't joke about some things. If gallows humor only works to distance ourselves from pain, then sincerely examining our situation moves us closer to the pain. Perhaps we need to acknowledge the pain in order to truly figure out what to do next.

I can't help but think of my generation of sarcastic cynics, mavens of irony, and worshipers of novelty (*I have a huge rare LP collection, I can go on for hours about obscure B-movies from the sixties, I have a mullet and wear a trucker hat even though I don't live in the country*). After witnessing our parents' generation become beaten, broken, and manipulated after trying so desperately to change the world, it makes perfect sense that my generation would end up broken and shattered and distant from meaning. The far-out hippies of yore gave birth to the cynical hipsters of today. When we can't stop devouring the world, who wants to look at the world we live in? Who wants to acknowledge the pain? We have given up. We have no hope for change nor the urge to create it. Why should we? Instead of tearing down civilization, we make sarcastic jokes about our predicament, further inculcating our apathy.

Meaninglessness vs. Rewilding

My mom asked today if I always feel either up or down or if I ever feel just a normal "humdrum." I told her that I never feel good if I don't follow my heart, that when I have to do something boring that I hate, over a long period of time, I always get depressed. Since I rarely have the opportunity to follow my heart in that way, I almost always feel depressed. She said that working a job she didn't like felt humdrum to her. I said it feels like terrible to me.

At the moment, I miss most of my friends in Portland. I miss drinking, club-hopping, dressing up, bumping into friends at bars, dancing, and feeling like part of something bigger. I wonder how much of all that filled sincere social needs or just worked to distract me from my deep-seated depression. The last time I felt this depressed, I ate a healthy paleo diet, exercised a ton, and didn't do any drugs. I did work at a shitty coffee shop wage-slave job while working my ass off trying to create a nonprofit that went nowhere.

I often have thoughts about suicide. It seems a lot easier than existing sometimes. I probably would have done it at age eleven (thinking of all those times I fell asleep with a knife at my wrist, eyes red and tired from crying myself to sleep) if I didn't feel a stronger need to save the world. I hate this feeling of meaninglessness. Hopelessness. Despair. The regular, all-too-familiar bouts of anxiety that feel like a knife up under the sternum and lungs full of water, drowning in grief. I think about all the factors: moving out of the inner city, losing frequent contact with my best friends, working a wage-slave job that doesn't use my best talents (even though I respect the company and support what they do), not speaking with my dad for seven months now. Add to all of that the weight of the world and the grief gets too heavy to carry. I slip and fall, and I have trouble standing back up.

I often say that I come to rewilding regardless of collapse, and I do. I also come to it because I strongly believe that it works to stop environmental destruction and restore it. I rewild because it works as a means to an end, whether that end means surviving collapse or creating a better way to live or both. But when I read about ice caps melting and methane and positive feedback loops of climate change, and that we can't change things now—that it will all melt and release methane that will heat up the planet and kill us all, wild or domestic—it makes me feel a kind of hopelessness and despair that I can barely articulate. While I no longer freak out about the apocalypse, I still have a ton of anxiety about the future. You won't find me screaming on the street corner, but you'll find me having trouble putting my clothes on in the morning. No matter how good or complete my life gets, no matter how much fun I have rewilding, I still struggle with a huge sense of impending doom and a feeling of meaninglessness.

On a large enough timeline, everything happening in this moment has no relevance to the whole of time. Some day the earth will merge with the sun, and everything alive today will have died long before. Does that make my life meaningless? If we look at life in a linear fashion, yes, it looks rather meaningless. If the methane heat apocalypse happens in twenty years, does that make this moment meaningless? In a linear sense, yes.

Civilizationists find purpose in progress, which they see as endless growth and expansion. We measure this progress with linear time, from "stone age" to "space age." I find meaning and purpose in maintaining quality relationships with humans and other-than-humans. Ironically I also perceive this purpose through linear time: from "domestic" to the eventual "wild." Most of the time rewilding still feels like a kind of progress to me. When I hear that I may never live a wild life because methane gas will make the planet so hot that we will all die, and that any "progress" towards creating cultures of rewilding will come to nothing, it feels meaningless.

Wild, animistic hunter-gatherers do not experience the maintaining of quality relationships in a linear fashion but in a cyclical one. This way of perceiving linear time vs. cyclical time feels to me like a crucial part of rewilding. If I don't see rewilding as a kind of progress, but rather the making and maintaining of relationships, it doesn't matter whether everyone burns up. Of course, that would suck and carries its own grief, but it doesn't lead to meaninglessness because life (depending on your definition of life), matter and energy, will continue. It feels difficult to see rewilding as nonprogressive, since we feel so strongly the chains of domestication, and moving away from that feels like progress towards an end goal of living wild. I would say that rewilding means maintenance and not progress. Even indigenous peoples spent their lives "rewilding," renewing their landscapes and psyches.

> Animism, because it seeks to relate and converse with the world, rather than to define and control it, always renews itself. It wakes up every morning fresh and alive, and every evening it tucks itself to

bed to dream again for the very first time. Since animism involves a relationship with the world, a living being that exists in the now, the present moment, what more relevant perspective could you find?

—Willem Larsen, *The College of Mythic Cartography*

These thoughts help me with meaninglessness as a concept, but they don't help me in the moment, because I still have to get up and carry the grief of civilization's devastation with me to my wage-slave job. I see few mourning for the collapse of salmon populations, though I spend hours sobbing over it, too sad or scared, frustrated, and hopeless to take action, legal or otherwise. Honestly I don't know how people make it through this fucked-up culture. I just don't. A best friend's death I can handle (for the most part). The death of the world? The threat of the death of the world? I don't think humans come into the world equipped to handle this kind of grief. That any of us wake up and continue to live should show us our beautiful inherent resilience (or our great ability to deny reality!).

I wish I knew how to get over depression, how to process all this grief. I wish sweat lodges, tinctures, Prozac, massages, acupuncture, alcohol, video games, television dramas, diets, and blogging did more than temporarily relieve me from the pain. I mean, I know that if I got paid to rewild I wouldn't feel as depressed. But I don't know how to get paid to rewild, aside from what I do now. Of course, not having to pay for clean water, a place to live and store things, and all of my food would kick ass too. I think this grief and depression will just exist until civilization comes down and the stress of this system no longer locks us into jobs we hate. I don't know.

Denial vs. Rewilding

> Who can live with a light heart while participating
> in a global slaughter that makes the Nazi holocaust
> look like a limbering-up exercise?
>
> —Daniel Quinn, *Providence*

The more time I spend at my job, the easier it becomes to ignore my pain. I can shut it off and let my body function. I can remove all external thought and simply become part of the machine, pushing a button over and over and over again, lulling my heart back to sleep with rhythmic clockwork.

I have heard that the key to meditation involves a repetitive motion, word, or phrase. I wonder if they mean something like this catchy little jingle from my early teens: "Hi, this is Peter with Moore Information, a public opinion research company. Could you spend a few moments on the phone with me to discuss some issues in your state?" Meditation helps you "transcend" your body, senses, and emotions (meaning it removes your humanity) so that you won't rise up to crush the system crushing you.

After days, weeks, months of this, I can simply forget about Urban Scout, collapse, and rewilding. I can bump my schedule up to five days a week. I can find "comfort" and "relaxation" in television shows like *Dancing with the Stars*, *Battlestar Galactica*, and cheap DVDs (four for $20) at the local video store. I can even have a couple beers or smoke a bowl. Then I can go to bed and get up the next morning and do it all over again. Let myself slide a little more. Focus on pushing the button, pulling the lever. Yes, sir. No, sir. Click, clack, click. If all I have to do involves pushing this little button, and I learn to focus on the button (a sort of meditation, if you will), then I can ignore my own pain. I can bury it.

I can wake up every morning and read the paper and believe that technology, the government, the scientists, or god will save us. I can bury the feeling deep down that any of this Urban Scout stuff ever happened. I could chalk it up to my more "radical" days as I sip on a can of cheap beer around the summer barbecue with the guys. "Ha ha, remember the ideological twenties?" On weekends I could work around the house, go fishing, go on a hike. Take my girl to dinner, the movies, and a bar. I could work on that novel, write some more music, play a few hours of the latest *Grand Theft Auto*, and plan what colors to paint the nursery. I could sell all those philosophical and anthropological books and field guides and download pop music MP3s to fill their place. I could forget their contents and fill the void with music loud enough to drown out any reminder of life before. I could read my voter's guide thoroughly and happily send in my ballot and believe in this culture again. I could make believe that things will work out. It wouldn't particularly feel that difficult...I've done this for most of my life. We all have.

I could pretend again that civilization and humanity mean the same thing. I could turn away from the horrors, slaves, and environmental decimation. I could forget that all the beauty civilization creates comes at the cost of destroying the world. I could forget about the thousands of indige-nous human cultures that created beauty, music, art, and culture and lived sustainably.

If ignorance equals bliss, then denial means feigning ignorance in order to feel blissful again.

I actually do watch *Dancing with the Stars* and *Battlestar Galactica* religiously. I play video games from time to time, go to the movies, take my girl out to dinner, and listen to punk rock at maximum volume. I have my vices and use them to relax from time to time, to escape when the pain feels beyond manageable. I also struggle with indulging the vices too much. Everyone has limits; everyone has a different level of support. I don't judge those who remain in denial, or who lose themselves in their addiction to civilization. I lose myself sometimes, so how can I judge those who don't have the support (we all need) to rewild? I use the support that I have to help support others. If this all works out, it will work because we have created a culture that supports rewilding. I grieve for those who remain in denial, who do not have the support to break the addiction, and I do my best to create a more supportive culture for people to break free. I also recognize that some people will die defending civilization. While I don't judge them, I still have no problem stopping them from destroying the planet.

But so too must we understand that the way of life that affords this kind of denial has already begun to unravel. Soon I won't have the choice to deny what our culture has done to this planet. No one will.

Instead of remaining in denial, I can continue to recognize that the way I live threatens every living thing on the planet, and the longer my civilized lifestyle lasts, the worse time we will all have in the coming years. I can acknowledge that civilization will not stop killing the planet. Call it what you want to call it: extraction of resources, progress, economic growth, manifest destiny, the holocaust, genocide. We all know the end product looks like the desert wasteland of the no-longer-fertile-crescent. I can allow myself to feel the pain rather than repress it into cancers, random acts of violence, alcoholism, and whatever else unmetabolized grief becomes.

You want the truth? I prefer grief to denial. At least grief acknowledges the horrors. I would rather contemplate suicide than blow away the truth in a hazy cloud of reefer smoke and video games. I don't see denial as the way out of grief. I don't see suicide as the way out of grief (though it seems easy when depressed). I live with depression from time to time and move through it with honesty, clarity, and solidarity with those who understand what civilization has done to us and feel it too. I welcome the grief with open arms.

People say I should focus on the more beautiful things in the world in order to feel better. But when I see a beautiful world, I also see our civilization destroying it. I have a loyal, supportive family and group of friends, and I also see civilization enslaving them. I have so many things to live for and feel great about, and I feel great about those things, and yet I also see the larger oppressive forces at work. None of these beautiful, amazing things will rescue me, and the rest of the world, from the clutches of civilization. When people in denial say "Focus on beautiful things," they really mean "Ignore the destruction." So while I have a lot to feel thankful for, I more often think about stopping the destruction and escaping slavery.

This helps me remember that I live as a slave, which reminds me that I don't enjoy living as a slave, which makes me not really enjoy life all that much in a general sense. I focus on the pain because you can only stop it by looking at it and figuring out what causes it. You don't fix your car engine by disconnecting the check engine light. Pain exists in order to motivate us to change our behavior, because the behavior threatens our survival. We need to look deeper. We need to see the beauty and recognize the destruction, simultaneously. Sometimes we need to escape and only look at the beauty, and sometimes we need to feel, full force, the horrors of civilization.

I feel like a pendulum, swinging back and forth from the horrors to the beauty to the horrors to the beauty. I have moments of despair and moments of escapism, and I try to strike enough balance to remove civilization from this planet. Eventually the pendulum stops swinging, becomes a balance beam—an edge.

Pessimism vs. Rewilding

For the most part I consider myself an optimist. I find it funny that a lot of people label me a pessimist because I advocate for the collapse of civilization. When I point out that civilization will collapse no matter what we do, rather than see that as an opportunity for something new, they file it away under doom and gloom. I think these people have it all backwards.

I have spent hours in fear of the collapse and imagining all the horrors of the apocalypse. But the more I study civilization, the more I realize that as long as it continues to grow, it will continue to devour the planet. As soon as it stops growing and begins to descend, life will reclaim and rewild the planet. In fact I can't think of a better set of descriptive words to refer to civilization than *doom and gloom*. The collapse signals *the end* of the doom and gloom caused by civilization and the rebirth of something sustainable.

You want to know what the apocalypse looks like? Go outside and look around. The apocalypse looks like alienation from your neighbors and family. It looks like eating food sprayed with toxins and then shipped 3,000 miles to the store. It looks like slaving your life away for mere pennies so you can afford another drink at the bar or puff on your pipe to forget about your slaving. Oh god, let's not put an end to any of that!

Martín Prechtel, a native who lived with post-civilization Mayans, explained that in his indigenous Mayan village the elders understood that the buildings in the village didn't make the community, the need for the buildings in the village created the community. For this reason, every year they would take their village down; when you have nothing, you need community. People helped each other rebuild their houses and in doing so strengthened their communities. They didn't build their houses to last because then they would have no reason, no need for their community. Martín saw his community shattered when the government forced people to build houses that would last. Nomadic people constantly broke down and dismantled their village and rebuilt it elsewhere. The end of civilization, the collapse, means the end of alienation and the rebirth of community. Geez, I feel like such a pessimist right now.

Fear of collapse works as a myth created by civilization in order to allow people to remain in denial and cling to the system. Civilization wants you to think you need structure, satellite TV, and loose-fit jeans, and that any life where you actually have to participate in the world will feel worse than the depression you currently struggle with. You want doom and gloom? The apocalypse came a long time ago. It just happened so slowly we didn't even notice.

I've seen a bumper sticker around town that says "No Farms, No Food." This just goes to show how people in civilization perceive subsistence. *Without farming, you'll starve!* Actually...you'll garden, hunt, gather, share, and trade with your neighbors. It may feel like more work than sitting at a laptop all day (like me right now), but it will feel great because your body expects and can easily handle that work.

This doom-and-gloom existential perception of collapse really only takes hold of people in "more developed" countries (meaning the countries that steal from everyone else). Rich people will no longer have the ability to steal from poor people. Doesn't that make you feel sooo sorry for those rich people?!? They won't have cheap IKEA crap filling their previously air-conditioned McMansion built by Mexicans. I can guarantee you that people in third world countries do not fear the collapse of civilization. Those at the bottom of the pyramid, the tortured slaves who make our affluent, luxurious American life possible, will no longer experience our oppression and will live more comfortable lives, restoring their connection to their landbase.

The horrors of civilized devastation and oppression will immediately lessen in most areas after the collapse. The rich will have the most difficulty coping, as will those who live in densely populated areas. Those in power, those used to living in McMansions and ordering take-out on their cell phones—those who sit at the top of the pyramid have the farthest to fall. They will feel discomfort as they adjust to a more normal, less decadent, less luxurious (at least in the civilized sense) life.

Call me a dreamer, but believing we can encourage collapse and rewild a dying planet feels like optimism to me.

Urban Scout vs. Rewilding

People have called me many names:

> Self-serving new-age nihilistic pseudo-hippie/yuppie quack-opportunist poseur-hipster-douchebag green-capitalist-bastard egotistical-celebrity-anarchist tool that gives everyone douchechills with a BS agenda, a trust fund from granny, and an obsession with publicity.

A poster of Meta-filter once asked, "Urban Scout, sincere crusader for sustainability or poseur-hipster-douchebag?"

Much of what I do involves performance art, so you could label me a poseur. I dress in (what I think look like) hip clothes, so you could call me a hipster. I often make egotistical jokes about myself and others, and I could see why someone would call me a douchebag. On top of that I sincerely teach rewilding skills to people and educate people on the ills of agriculture. My life revolves around teaching sustainability. So you could call me a sincere crusader for sustainability. Can't I have all of these qualities simultaneously? This "one or the other" mentality reflects back to Aristotle's "is" of identity; you can only "be" A or B, not both. So you can just go ahead and call me a poseur-hipster-douchebag, sincerely crusading for sustainability.

This question, though intellectually incoherent, haunts me because of the sheer number of people who attack me using this Aristotelian logic. Most often people say that I "talk" more than I "walk" without thinking about the importance and need for talking about things. People need to understand this stuff. I get off on thinking about this stuff and writing about it. I don't think of myself as a martyr sacrificing myself for the greater good or carrying some burden. It really upsets me when people don't see the value of talking about things. I keep talking because of the shit I see in the media projecting a fucked-up worldview.

George Bush Jr. said during his 2008 State of the Union Address:

> America is leading the fight against global hunger. Today, more than half the world's food aid comes from the United States. And tonight, I ask Congress to support an innovative proposal to provide food assistance by purchasing crops directly from farmers in the developing world, so we can *build up local agriculture and help break the cycle of famine.* (Audience applause.) [Emphasis added.]

If we really want to "fight" third world hunger we would leave them the fuck alone, not teach/force them to practice the very pestilence that brought their culture and landbase to its knees to begin with. If Americans really wanted to stop population growth they would not provide "food aid" but landbase rejuvenation. Not to mention that initiatives to buy food from 3,000 miles away in third world countries make us more dependent on foreign food sources. So much for the "locavore" movement!

I can't help but think, doesn't everyone know that agriculture *causes* famine? As time passes and things get worse,

I keep forgetting the complete lack of even the simplest ecological understanding making its way up the pyramid. This doesn't look good for the planet...

The February 2008 *National Geographic* contains a cover story on the "Black Pharaohs of Egypt." Throughout the article we see the scary desertscape of Egypt: sand without soil. Does anyone ever wonder why? No, because we would rather talk about "Black Pharaohs" than ecological genocide. Then we would have to face what we currently do to the planet. Doesn't discussing the race of past civilizations' rulers sound so much more interesting? I mean, imagine a ruler in your head. Now imagine they have black skin. Crazy, right?!? Have I ever mentioned how much I hate this culture?

On one page we see an advertisement for a special *National Geographic* television program on "climate change." The following page contains an advertisement for chips. It depicts three rows of crops: potatoes, corn, and wheat.

Next to eat crop we see a particular bag of chips made from the crop. The tag line: "The best snacks on earth." Do you see the irony here? An advertisement for agricultural crops that cause deforestation and desertification wedged between photographs of desert landscapes devoid of life created by older civilizations and a special television program on the problems we face because of climate change, which we contributed to through deforesting the planet. No doubt many people sit in horror as they watch the ice caps melt before their eyes and the last polar bear drown on their televisions, all the while snacking on a bag of Sun Chips.

No one has any fucking idea why civilization causes a loss of biodiversity, desertification, and climate change. They don't even think about food subsistence. They believe that humans practice agriculture just like we breathe the air. We cannot question it because we can't see the link. Our ability to see through civilization's agricultural propaganda and rewild will determine whether we survive the collapse as individuals, communities, and as a species.

What, no applause?

If we want to rewild the planet and create sustainable cultures, we need people spreading the ideology of rewilding in order to offset the effects of civilization. Marketing the sustainable worldview of rewilding fills probably 95% of what I do. If rewilding meant running away to the wilderness—which it doesn't—it wouldn't have much of an impact on many people. The more people turned on to rewilding, the softer the crash, because it means more people focused on dismantling civilization and restoring the biodiversity of their bioregion.

Though marketing rewilding fills most of my time, this doesn't mean I don't walk my talk, since cultures have many members who serve different functions. Just because I don't focus on medicinal plants doesn't mean I don't walk my talk. Just because some people-who-rewild don't care to know how to tan hides or build bow-drill fires doesn't mean they don't walk their talk. It takes a village. It takes people promoting and tending to the culture. It takes people building the boat for the rewilding culture to sail in. Whether you call it ideology, mythology, propaganda, marketing, or worldview, those elements form the frame of the cultural rewilding boat. Understanding ways of living that promote biodiversity (and ways of living that don't) forms the foundation of rewilding cultures. You can't build cultural foundations with your hands; you build with your words, observations, and stories.

Some people work as frame builders for the boat; others learn to navigate the oceans once in the boat. Most people focus on one thing but do a little of everything. If you really understand how talking fits into culture building, thinking of people as talkers and walkers makes no sense: talkers and walkers do not exist. People serve different functions, all talkers, all walkers.

We can't have culture without stories. If we want a new culture, we need lots of stories. Hundreds. Thousands. Millions. We need to outcompete civilization's propaganda. When I see hundreds of thousands of people rewilding, telling their own stories, I'll know that I have done my job well. When I have hundreds of friends rewilding in my bioregion, serving their own roles in the culture, I'll know that I have done my job well and will feel happy that I have a culture to support me. Hopefully they'll recognize all of the foundational work that I have done to make the culture happen.

Everything vs. Rewilding

Rewilding doesn't refer to a way of dressing, or a cool new diet, or a sustainable product you can use to fuel your car, or voting with dollars, or any of that. It refers to a way of living that requires an entirely new way of looking at the world. Before you can physically rewild, you need to see the world through the eyes of the wild, which means seeing it in contrast to that which domesticates: civilization. When most people have no awareness of their own domestication, have never viewed their civilized lives in relation to wild ones, they will not understand rewilding and will simply replicate civilization with more primitive tools than we use today.

Once we understand the fundamental picture of civilization, we can hold up rewilding next to anything and see the civilization in it. Once we see the civilization in something, we can rewild it. Civilization does not have a monopoly on music, art, language, violence, or irony. We can use those tools, too, through the lens of rewilding. My friend Chris thought of a good metaphor for it:

> There's a Huge Pink Elephant in the room that no one seems to talk about, and it's (what's the quote from *Princess Mononoke*?) a Big Huge Slimy Life-Sucking Monster of Death called Civilization. I love permaculture and regenerative design, and those are the folks I'll talk to when I want to figure

out how to garden my yard, or how to inhabit my land with my community more sustainably. But what about that little problem of civilization? Seventy-five species a day—gone. Ninety thousand acres of forest a day—gone. Thirteen and a half million tons of CO_2 a day into the atmosphere—fuck! That's civilization. What I hear Scout saying is simply, "But let's talk about that too!" And specifically—in what ways does not directly addressing that elephant's presence influence us when we get into our permaculture design, or regenerative design, or ecovillage planning, or re-souling work, or whatever? For me, it's pretty significant to look around and think, "We really can't do this good stuff for real with all this here. With all of us here. Only a small amount of what's here now can be here and have this work." I would rather not notice that, and feel good about buying my heritage seeds and my commercially produced organic compost. But the more I take an interest in the long view—"How is this really going to play out and work out?"—the more I see that elephant sitting there, shitting on everything (no offense to elephants), and there's just not enough room. I like the "vs." to the extent that it gets us to look up from what we're doing (regardless of how friendly that activity might be to rewilding) and ask, "Yeah, and how exactly are we addressing the elephant as we do this?"

Rewilding means much more than simply "undoing domestication." But we need to see how civilization domesticates us in order to rewild. We need to see the elephant so that we can make sure to kill it. (Sorry, Dumbo.) Rewilding begins with seeing the civilization, the empire, the systems of domination in everything that we do, so that we can uncivilize it together.

Rewilding vs. Rewilding

I have to say that by now, after spending years philos-
ophizing about the word *rewilding*...I fucking hate it. I
know that sounds ridiculous. I've thought a lot about the
errors in choosing the word to describe what I do. Two
things in particular come to mind:

1. The misconception of *wild.* No matter how hard I
   try, it seems people just don't understand that wild
   doesn't mean "un-managed by humans." This gives
   way to people using the term *rewilding* as a synonym
   for primitive skills, simple living, and all kinds of
   seventies hippie crap. No matter how many ways
   we define rewilding, the misconception of *wild* will
   always have its presence and always work as a barrier
   to quick understanding.

2. The preexisting scientific definition. Scientists have
   their own kind of rewilding, Pleistocene rewilding,
   which involves habitat restoration and excludes humans. This also causes a lot of confusion when people
   think I mean to reintroduce elephants and other large
   mammals into North America. No...I don't mean that.

From the beginning, *rewilding* already had several uses.
Trying to get people to rally behind a concept or idea
using a preexisting term with several definitions doesn't
make it easy to catch on and causes lots of confusion along
the way. Whoops!

Anytime you give an idea a name, you simultaneously give it power and kill its ability to change. It becomes a term, set in stone. The term itself can catch on, grow a bigger following. But the evolution of the idea that created the term stops. Once you have a doctrine, a written concept, it feels increasingly difficult to change. We see this with languages. As soon as a language has a dictionary, it becomes set in stone and ceases to have any fluidity. The book becomes the overall authority on a subject instead of the people speaking the language. This happened to rewilding the moment it became a word. Of course, to get people up to speed, you must talk about it. Spread it. And thus the power in giving it a name. Eventually it will become obsolete, and someone else will give a name to what rises in its place. And so on.

For the last year I have debated with myself whether or not to publish this work. For as soon as my current thoughts sit on this page, they seem to represent a kind of permanence that I don't feel I can shake. Ten years from now I will not agree with a lot of the things I wrote here. I know this. More experiences, deeper levels of connection, will make me eat my own words. I know this, but does the reader know? The reader may read this and see it as a representation of what I believe currently, ten years after print, twenty years after print. Forty years from now someone might say, "Urban Scout believes X," when in fact I don't. Things change. I want to make it clear that everything in this book I hold up in the air, in a space that I can change and probably will in time.

Similarly, in the future I may not think of what I do as "rewilding" as described in this book. Whatever I do, whether I call it rewilding now and snugufunpoling in ten years, doesn't matter. What I have hoped to convey in this book doesn't represent a word but a trajectory. So what does that mean? It means…fuck rewilding. Fuck this book. Stay true to the fluidity of the trajectory behind the word. If *rewilding*, the word, changes to mean something other than this trajectory I have described, then most certainly I would not identify with it. I identify with the trajectory: a non-appropriated, authentic, regenerative, indigenous life.

The Rewild Frontier

No one knows what the future will bring, but this we know: civilizations destroy the land. Our civilization won't last much longer. A movement known as rewilding has started against civilization. This movement has a frontier, and we live on it.

We generally refer to forces of nature as forces out of human control. We cannot control which direction the wind blows, we cannot stop fields from turning into forests, we cannot stop the earth from spinning around the sun. I believe that culture functions in a homologous manner: a force of nature out of our control.

Often we hear the debate over whether human behavior comes more from our nature or our nurture. But I never hear people say that no difference exists between the two. That these elements have separate names gives rise to a meaningless discussion that only serves to keep us from understanding how we can relate to the world. If we believe that nurturing somehow exists separately from our nature, we believe that we have some amount of control over our own nature. This means that the term *nurture* describes the systems we have in place to control behavior, where our nature looks like something outside our system of control. I believe that these systems of control come from our nature. If systems for controlling behavior come from our nature as socially organized animals, our nature involves nurturing and our nurturing does not separate itself from our nature. Our nature involves nurturing. Got it?

I don't think many people (besides genetic engineers) would argue if I said that our nature lies out of our hands. Humans have characteristics brought about through evolution. Our behavior varies from strategy to strategy of living with this nature. We could say that the culture (our real "nurturer") controls us, that myths or memes dictate how we behave and what decisions we make. But above culture, above nurture, lies nature, the environment, and the natural laws of the planet. Although our nature involves nurturing, our strategies for how we nurture, how we create cultural behavior, dictate themselves through the environment in which we live. We have no control over the forces, or systems of nature, only strategies for living with them. Those strategies shape themselves according to environmental systems. Because we have no control over environmental systems, in a sense we have no control over the cultural systems that adapt to them. We only have the power to adapt to environmental changes: the ability to change with the environment, not change the environment to live with us. People must respond to environmental changes or they will die.

I refer to this process as "the power of need." Needs make the world go round. People need food to live, so they hunt and gather. People need sex to proliferate, create culture, and feel good, so they have sex. Needs can feel physical, like the need to eat or sleep. Needs can feel emotional, like the need to feel supported. Needs can feel mythological or spiritual, like the need to go to heaven or the need to feel useful to a greater group. None of these needs have the same immediacy as the need for water. A friend of mine refers to this phenomenon (force of nature) as "the brown water effect," meaning people will not take up arms until they have brown water pouring out their faucets. When the culture cannot meet the direct survival needs of its people, you cannot have a culture. We need clean water to live. Duh!

When Rachel Carson wrote *Silent Spring*, she began a cultural movement of environmentalists who foresaw the coming brown water. At this point most people (in America at least) have clean tap water, aside from chlorine, chloramine, fluoride, arsenic, etc. (uh, never mind...I guess they have water that looks and tastes clean). Even though they have seen the film *An Inconvenient Truth* and have an awareness of the "climate crisis," they still have clean tap water, air-conditioning, Internet access, cell phones, SUVs, McDonalds, Saturday morning cartoons, happy hour specials, and HBO. As long as this culture continues to provide these privileged distractions, only a subculture of people with the wits to see and the heart to feel will look for alternative strategies like rewilding.

Rewilding doesn't just mean learning about edible plants and how to make buckskin. I can stand around here all I want and identify plants and tell stories and have babies, and still the world will die at the hands of the civilized. Still civilization will meet me with outward violence as it collapses. As long as civilization holds its monopoly on violence and control, as long as the wildfire has fuel to burn, abandoning the system of civilization for something else remains a problem. Many laws exist to prevent people from rewilding: hunting and gathering and gardening fees, regulations, restrictions, and taxes that make self-sufficiency through rewilding a hard game to play, especially for a family. Breaking the law (civilization's threat of violence) works as an inevitable step in creating a rewilding culture and surviving the collapse of civilization. Rewilding also means fighting back. With fuel to burn, a wildfire will gain in momentum and appear unstoppable. However, it becomes very easy to put out a wildfire after it passes the point of diminishing returns. With no more fuel to burn, it begins to die.

In order to fight back against civilization, we need to have lives worth fighting for. Indigenous peoples who fought against civilization had something we civilized people don't: a connection to land and family worth fighting for, worth killing for. Hunter-gatherers fought for the land and lifestyle and culture that they had for millions of years, because it gave them life. They had a system that worked and that they defended. They fought side by side with their brothers and sisters and uncles and cousins and grandfathers and grandmothers, both humans and other-than-human. We have nothing like that: no familial, supportive, life-giving culture to fight for nor to care for us as we succeed in bringing down civilization. Unless we simply feel suicidal, we need lives worth fighting for. Rewilding means reclaiming a life worth living and defending it against those who wish to domesticate it.

Often we hear *lifeboat* used to describe these plans for surviving through collapse. I prefer not to use that word, as lifeboats merely suggest a temporary safe place. We want to abandon the ship for a new one, better than the one we left, not something small and temporary. Noah didn't build his ark as a lifeboat; he built it as a boat big enough for every living thing in the world. Rewilding cultures should have no less space.

In the story of rewilding we have three acts: early collapse, deep in collapse, and after collapse. In the first act we need to develop an escape plan from the barriers that hold us captive to civilization. The second act involves living a life worth fighting for as we hold our ground and encourage the collapse along. In the third act we will celebrate the end of civilization and continue to rewild all of the places that civilization has domesticated. I see a whole cast of characters working here. I see people rewilding outside of civilization's control, holding their own. I see people on the borders of the rewild frontier, pushing civilization into retreat where its weak spots exist. I see people in the lion's den, rewilding right in the middle of civilization. I see an "underground rewild-road" of sorts, helping those in civilization escape to wild areas.

Of course, rewilding doesn't mean that you have to confront civilization head on. Not everyone in a culture takes the role of the warrior. We need nurturers and healers and mothers and fathers and everything else. Just have clarity about whether you've chosen a different role based on fear of living as a warrior, and don't disguise that fear as pacifist ideology or condemn those who have no fear and live as front-line warriors. As a warrior, remember not to let the fight against civilization get in the way of living—make it part of a whole life of rewilding. What else do we have to fight for but our loved ones, human and other-than-human? To fight back, I need a life worth living, and to me that means having children and growing a family and learning to hunt and gather and give back to the land and kicking civilization's ass for my family and rewilding cultures.

The rewild frontier looks similar to the civilized frontier, only backward: we will see people stop tilling the soil, stop farming, and start encouraging succession. We will see violence as the civilized try to resist those-who-rewild. Rather than see the wild retreat from civilization, we will see civilization retreat from the wild until one day we will see civilization no more.

Go out there and start rewilding now. Plant an orchard. Protect wild lands. Teach your children that "weeds" don't exist. Talk with other-than-humans. Talk with humans. Shut down the grid. Learn to hunt and trap without modern tools. Take out roads. Make a family. Turn a deerskin into buckskin. Hold your ground. Make friends. Discover enemies. Reclaim land from civilization. Get really fucking angry. Relax. Cry. Laugh. Follow your heart, follow your heart, follow your heart, and live a life worth living, worth remembering, worth mythologizing until the sun engulfs the planet.

You have a choice: rewild or die.

Bibliography

Anderson, M. Kat. *Tending the Wild: Native American Knowledge and the Management of California's Natural Resources.* Berkeley, California: University of California Press, 2005.

Anthony, David W. *The Horse, The Wheel, and Language: How Bronze-Age Riders from the Eurasian Steppes Shaped the Modern World.* Princeton, New Jersey: Princeton University Press, 2007.

Apostol, Dean, and Marcia Sinclair. *Restoring the Pacific Northwest: The Art and Science of Ecological Restoration in Cascadia.* Washington, D.C.: Island Press, 2006.

Basso, Keith H. *Wisdom Sits in Places: Landscape and Language Among the Western Apache.* Albuquerque, New Mexico: University of New Mexico Press, 1996.

Bourland, D. David. *To Be or Not: An E-Prime Anthology.* San Francisco: International Society for General Semantics, 1991.

Boyd, Robert. *Indians, Fire, and the Land in the Pacific Northwest.* Corvallis, Oregon: Oregon State University Press, 1999.

Brown, Tom Jr. *The Tracker: The Story of Tom Brown, Jr.* Englewood Cliffs, New Jersey: Prentice-Hall, 1978.

———. *The Vision: The Dramatic True Story of One*

Man's Search for Enlightenment. New York: Berkley Books, 1988.

Campbell, Joseph. *The Hero with a Thousand Faces.* New York: Pantheon Books, 1949.

———. *The Power of Myth.* New York: Doubleday, 1988.

Cordain, Loren. *The Paleo Diet: Lose Weight and Get Healthy by Eating the Food You Were Designed to Eat.* New York: J. Wiley, 2002.

Deur, Douglas, and Nancy J. Turner, eds. *Keeping It Living: Traditions of Plant Use and Cultivation on the Northwest Coast of North America.* Seattle: University of Washington Press, 2005.

Diamond, Jared. *Collapse: How Societies Choose to Fail or Succeed.* New York: Viking, 2005.

Elpel, Thomas J. *Botany in a Day: Thomas J. Elpel's Herbal Field Guide to Plant Families.* Pony, Montana: HOPS Press, 2000.

Gatto, John Taylor. *Dumbing Us Down: The Hidden Curriculum of Compulsory Schooling.* Philadelphia: New Society Publishers, 1992.

———. *The Underground History of American Education.* Oxford, New York: Oxford Village Press, 2001.

Griffin. Sky. *Reclaim, Rewild.* Self-published zine. 2004

Godesky, Jason. *The Thirty Theses.* 2006. http://theanarchistlibrary.org/library/jason-godesky-thirty-theses.

Gowdy, John. *Limited Wants, Unlimited Means: A Reader on Hunter-Gatherer Economics and the Environment.* Washington, D.C.: Island Press, 1998.

Harrison, Owen. *Open Space Technology: A User's Guide.* San Francisco: Berrett-Koehler Publishers, 1997.

Harvey, Graham. *Animism: Respecting the Living World.* New York: Columbia University Press, 2006.

Hemenway, Toby. *Gaia's Garden: A Guide to Home-Scale Permaculture.* White River Junction, Vermont: Chelsea Green, 2001.

Heinberg, Richard. *The Primitivist Critique of Civilization.* Paper presented at the 24th annual meeting of the International Society for the Comparative Study of Civilizations at Wright State University, Dayton, Ohio, June 15, 1995.

Holt, John. *How Children Learn.* New York: Pitman, 1967.

———. *Teach Your Own: A Hopeful Path for Education.* New York: Delacorte Press, Seymour Lawrence, 1981.

Jensen, Derrick. *A Language Older Than Words.* New York: Context Books, 2000.

———. *The Culture of Make Believe.* New York : Context Books, 2002.

———. *Welcome to the Machine: Science, Surveillance, and the Culture of Control.* White River Junction, Vermont: Chelsea Green, 2004.

———. *Endgame.* 2 vols. New York: Seven Stories Press, 2006.

———. *As the World Burns: 50 Simple Things You Can Do to Stay in Denial.* New York: Seven Stories Press, 2007.

Kane, Joe. *Savages.* New York: Knopf, 1995.

Keith, Lierre. *The Vegetarian Myth: Food, Justice, and Sustainability.* Crescent City, California: Flashpoint Press, 2009.

Korzybski, Alfred. *Science and Sanity: An Introduction to*

Non-Aristotelian Systems and General Semantics.
Lancaster, Pennsylvania: Science Press Printing, 1933.

Larsen, Willem. *The College of Mythic Cartography:
2004–2013.* Portland, Oregon: Willem Larsen, 2014.

Liebenberg, Louis. *The Art of Tracking: The Origin of
Science.* Claremont, South Africa: D. Philip, 1990.

Liedloff, Jean. *The Continuum Concept.* London:
Duckworth, 1975.

Llewellyn, Grace. *The Teenage Liberation Handbook: How
to Quit School and Get a Real Life and Education.*
Eugene, Oregon: Lowry House, 1991.

Mann, Charles C. *1491: New Revelations of the Americas
Before Columbus.* New York: Knopf, 2005.

Manning, Richard. *Against the Grain: How Agriculture
Has Hijacked Civilization.* New York: North Point
Press, 2005.

Montgomery, David. *Dirt: The Erosions of Civilization.*
Oakland: University of California Press, 2007.

Mowat, Farley. *People of the Deer.* Boston: Little, Brown,
1952.

———. *Never Cry Wolf.* Boston: Little, Brown, 1963.

Ortiz, Beverly R. *It Will Live Forever: Traditional Yosemite
Indian Acorn Preparation.* Berkeley, California:
Heyday Books, 1991.

Prechtel, Martín. *Secrets of the Talking Jaguar: A Mayan
Shaman's Journey to the Heart of the Indigenous Soul.*
New York: Jeremy P. Tarcher, 1998.

———. *Long Life, Honey in the Heart: A Story of
Initiation and Eloquence from the Shores of a Mayan
Lake.* New York: Jeremy P. Tarcher, 1999.

————. *Disobedience of the Daughter of the Sun: A Mayan Tale of Ecstasy, Time, and Finding One's True Form.* Berkeley, California: North Atlantic Books, 2005.

————. *Stealing Benefacio's Roses.* Berkeley, California: North Atlantic Books, 2006.

Quinn, Daniel. *Ishmael.* New York: Bantam/Turner Book, 1992.

————. *The Story of B.* New York: Bantam Books, 1996.

————. *My Ishmael.* New York: Bantam Books, 1997.

————. *Beyond Civilization: Humanity's Next Great Adventure.* New York: Harmony Books, 1999.

————. *The Tales of Adam.* Hanover, New Hampshire: Steerforth Press, 2005.

Quinn, Daniel, and Alan D. Thornhill. *Food Production and Population Growth: Why the Greatest Crisis in Human History Is Being Faced in OUR Generation.* Audio. New Tribal Ventures, 1998.

Rezendez, Paul. *Tracking and the Art of Seeing: How to Read Animal Tracks and Sign.* Charlotte, Vermont: Camden House, 1992.

Staments, Paul. *Mycelium Running: How Mushrooms Can Help Save the World.* Berkeley, California: Ten Speed Press, 2005.

Stewart, Hilary. *Indian Fishing: early methods on the Northwest Coast.* Seattle: University of Washington Press, 1977.

————. *Cedar: Tree of Life to the Northwest Coast Indians.* Seattle: University of Washington Press, 1984.

————. *Stone, Bone, Antler and Shell: Artifacts of the*

Northwest Coast. 2nd ed. Seattle: University of Washington Press, 1996.

Stewart, Omer. *Forgotten Fires: Native Americans and the Transient Wilderness.* Norman, Oklahoma: University of Oklahoma Press, 2002.

Suttles, Wayne, and William Sturtevant, eds. *Handbook of North American Indians.* Vol. 7, Northwest Coast. Washington, D.C.: Smithsonian Institution, 1990.

Turner, Nancy. *The Earth's Blanket: Traditional Teachings for Sustainable Living.* Seattle: University of Washington Press, 2005.

Wescott, David, ed. *Primitive Technology: A Book of Earth Skills.* From the Society of Primitive Technology. Salt Lake City, Utah: Gibbs Smith Publisher, 1999.

Young, Jon. *Seeing Through Native Eyes: Understanding the Language of Nature.* Audio. Santa Cruz, California: OWLink Media, 1996.

Young, Jon, and Ellen Haas. *The Art of Mentoring and Coyote Teaching.* Audio. Santa Cruz, California: OWLink Media, 1997.

Zerzan, John. *Future Primitive: and Other Essays.* Williamsburg, Brooklyn, New York: Autonomedia, 1994.

Zerzan, John, ed. *Against Civilization: Readings and Reflections.* Port Townsend, Washington: Feral House, 2005.

———— ed. *Green Anarchy Issue #16: Rewilding Primer.* Eugene, OR: Green Anarchy, 2004.

About the Author

I consider myself a multi-disciplinary artist and environ-mental educator. I'm a fourth-generation Portlander. My first merit badge in the Boy Scouts was for basketry. From there I went on to receive the esteemed rank of Eagle Scout. It was during my years camping with the scouts that I began to yearn for a deeper connection to place. At the age of sixteen, inspired by Daniel Quinn's *Ishmael*, I dropped out of high school and ran away from home to travel across the United States and attend Tom Brown Jr.'s Tracking, Nature Observation and Wilderness Survival School in New Jersey. After that I went to Wilderness Awareness School in Washington State, where I attended several Art of Mentoring workshops led by Jon Young. I have been heavily influenced by the works of Joseph Campbell, Derrick Jensen, Nancy Turner, Douglas Deur, M. Kat Anderson, Finisia Medrano, and Martín Prechtel. I began blogging about rewilding under the moniker Urban Scout in 2004. Between 2004 and 2008, I received local press in *The Oregonian*, *Portland Mercury*, and *Willamette Week*, national press in *ReadyMade*, and international press in *Positive Living* (UK) and *Chain Reaction* (AU) for my efforts to create and promote the culture of rewilding.

In 2007 I created rewild.com, an international online forum dedicated to discussions about rewilding. In 2008 I published a collection of my blogs in the first edition of *Rewild or Die*. In 2009, after dedicating so much time to writing and managing rewild.com, I founded Rewild

Portland, a nonprofit organization with the mission of creating cultural and environmental resilience through the education of earth-based arts, traditions, and technologies. I love basketry, I play the banjo, and I am a fluent speaker of Chinuk Wawa (aka Chinook Jargon), the Native trade language of the Pacific Northwest and heritage language of the Confederated Tribes of Grand Ronde. During the summer of 2012 I attended Lynx Vilden's Stone Age immersion program. I've been an environmental educator since the early 2000s, working with local organizations like Cascadia Wild, Friends of Tryon Creek, Audubon Society, Portland Waldorf School, Shining Star Waldorf School, and Cleveland High School, and I currently serve as executive director of Rewild Portland.

A production of Rewild Portland
http://www.rewildportland.com/

Lightning Source UK Ltd.
Milton Keynes UK
UKHW021819010323
417874UK00010B/398

9 781621 069720